The Lion's Bridge

A GIRL'S LIFE IN HITLER'S WURZBURG

Rosemarie Scheller Rowan

Bloomington, IN Milton Keynes, UK

authorHOUSE™

AuthorHouse™
1663 Liberty Drive, Suite 200
Bloomington, IN 47403
www.authorhouse.com
Phone: 1-800-839-8640

AuthorHouse™ UK Ltd.
500 Avebury Boulevard
Central Milton Keynes, MK9 2BE
www.authorhouse.co.uk
Phone: 08001974150

First published by AuthorHouse 6/23/2006

ISBN: 1-4259-3720-9 (sc)

Library of Congress Control Number: 2006906053

Printed in the United States of America
Bloomington, Indiana

This book is printed on acid-free paper.

Forward

My mother wrote all the words you are about to read. I'm just the editor and I didn't have to do much of that. I'm also my mother's eldest son. Mom grew up in war-torn Germany in a charming and beautiful city called Wurzburg, in the winemaking region of Bavaria. She had a very special relationship with her sister Karin and their dream was to record their memoirs together. It was something they were going to do together in the same way they had spent their early years, and stayed together in spirit all their lives.

Sadly, Aunt Karin passed away several years ago before they had a chance to start this project and I know it was the hardest thing my mother ever had to bear. She wrote what follows to help with the grieving for her dear sister. It was her therapy and she wrote this in Aunt Karin's memory and in her honor. She told me that she wrote it to keep Karin's memory alive. Something I will always remember about my Aunt Karin is that she always looked at me with such loving eyes. This is dedicated to her.

Mom also wrote this to honor the memory of her mother and father—my Oma and Opa—who had to struggle all their lives, through two world wars in an effort to try and make a better life for their children. They did a wonderful job. My mother is an extraordinary woman. She also wrote this for us, her children and her grandchildren so we would all have a better appreciation for what life was like in those times, those times in the lives of what Mr. Tom Brokaw has termed our greatest generation.

One day, about four years ago, I was at my parents' home in Melbourne, Florida and my Mom gave me this little composition book and asked me to read what she had written in it. The book was filled with her tiny, hand written printing and I marveled at the work she had done. I had no idea that she could write so well and I was amazed at how well she could recall so much of her youngest years in such detail.

It was nearly Thanksgiving at the time and Florida had just gone through a particularly devastating hurricane season. Their home had sustained some damage and here I was holding a treasure in my hands that had no real way of being shared with anyone else and could easily be blown away in the next storm. I asked Mom if I could take it home with me and she reluctantly agreed. I think she feared something might happen to it on my flight back home.

I decided to begin typing what she had written to preserve it and make it easier to share with the rest of the family and that first "installment" turned out to be over fifty typed pages. I made copies for everyone in the family, punched holes in them and bound them in three ring binders and sent them off as part of my Christmas present to everyone.

It was a huge hit within the family. Everyone could now read what Mom had written and share our thoughts and impressions of it. The next year, Mom has another composition book filled with her writing so off I went to typing again and off went another installment to everyone just in time for Christmas.

And the next year, it was the same as the last except with one difference. We now had these three ring binders filled with over one hundred pages of Mom's life story—at least through the war's end—and other people were asking to read them. And when they did, the overwhelming response was that we should find a way to publish them.

So here I am talking with you and sharing how all this came about. Whenever you go to publish something, the publisher and the readers like it to have some sort of title. The original binders I sent out were entitled, "The Memoirs of Rosemarie Scheller." This was fine for us family members, but I wanted to give it something a little more compelling.

One of the most beautiful and notable features of Wurzburg is the Lion's Bridge crossing the Main River. When we lived in Germany we walked across it many times and on the far side were the hillsides covered with vineyards, and the Marienberg Castle sitting majestically astride one of the highest hills.

The bridge featured daily in Mom's life and could be seen from the apartment windows where they lived. And it was where the family all gathered and held each other during the firestorm that razed Wurzburg in those wretched, waning days of the war. It was an impressive structure to her as a small child and I thought it made a fine title for what Mom had written.

It is not an easy thing to get something published and I was fortunate to find the good folks at AuthorHouse. I would like to express my appreciation to them for helping us bring Mom's life to print. I would also like to thank my sisters and my brother for their insights and help in getting these memoirs to this point. And I would like to thank my cousin Linda whose mother this book is dedicated to. Most of all, we all have someone very special, very extraordinary to thank for this. Thank you Mom. I love you.

Wallace M. Rowan, Jr.
March 18, 2006

One

Karola woke up to the sound of a baby crying. She lay there listening for a while. Somehow it sounded different than before. Then she realized that she wasn't alone in her bed. Karin, her fifteen-month old baby sister was sleeping soundly beside her. This was really strange now because Karin was supposed to be in Mama's room in the crib next to Mama's bed.

Why was there a baby crying in Mama's room when Karin wasn't even in there? Who was that baby? Somehow she got that sinking feeling and it wasn't long before her suspicions were confirmed. Another baby sister had been born right around six o'clock that morning, March 23, 1934.

All she could think of was, "Oh no, not another one." She had been the only child for well over seven and a half years and was the apple of Mama and Papa's eyes. Their whole world centered around "das Kind," (the child) as they called her. Of course, there were pitfalls to being an only child too. Like so many new parents, Mama and Papa just wanted to make sure they were bringing her up right and in the process probably were stricter with her than necessary.

Mama was not quite twenty years old when she had Karola. Papa was five years older. Neither one knew much about children. But they knew they wanted their child to have a better life than they had had. They had no money or very, very little.

Papa worked as a shoe repairman in a leather goods shop. He had learned to be a shoemaker and could create a pair of shoes from scratch, but mass production came along and that was the end of his shoemaking. He could take an old pair of shoes with rundown heels and holes in the soles and make them look like new again, which is what he did, day in and day out.

Unfortunately, there wasn't any money in it. People would bring shoes to be repaired and then wouldn't pick them up, especially around Christmas. So the shopkeeper would be unable to pay the workers. This happened quite often, but somehow they managed anyway to make the holidays special, especially Christmas.

They decorated their first Christmas tree with gold and silver walnuts that they had carefully cracked, taken the meat out, glued back together and painted. They also blew out eggs through little holes on each end, cleaned them and decorated them with foil paper stars from candy bars. Those were their first Christmas tree decorations.

For Karola's present they took an old flat-bottom wicker basket, attached some broomstick legs and some wheels Papa had found and created an adorable doll buggy. Mama loved to sew and made all the bedding for it, and they got her a doll.

At that time they owned a very gentle cat named Molly, who got at least as many rides in the buggy as the doll did. Karola would put a bonnet on the cat and lay her in the buggy on her back, cover her up with just her little face and paws sticking out, just like a baby. Those were the good days, but then there were bad ones too.

Karola was kind of clumsy. Just walking along, she would stumble and fall on her head, which promptly would make a big knot on her forehead every time. This would happen so quickly, Mama couldn't stop it. Then Papa would get really mad and accuse Mama of not watching her closely enough. He was worried that "the Child" would suffer brain damage.

Then there was the trouble with eating. The Child just didn't want to eat. But she had to sit there until every crumb was gone. Quite often it was just some old dry bread with something on it like cheese or so, which really was a lot to chew for a little girl.

Meat was another problem. Karola just didn't like it. Not that they had a lot of it. Meat was a treat that was mainly eaten only on Sundays in those days. So, when they had some, they made sure that the Child ate some too, even if it was a battle. She managed to grow and even thrive in spite of getting terrible diseases like whooping cough, double pneumonia, measles and countless others.

One feat proved what a resourceful little girl she really was. It was the winter of 1928/29, one of the coldest on record ever. The Main River was completely frozen over, so you could walk all the way across it—something that had never happened before in anyone's memory.

Everyone stayed in as much as possible, trying to keep warm by their little coal stoves. But the winter seemed endless and relentless and eventually Mama and Karola had to venture out into the bitter cold to go to the market and get more supplies. This involved going up Landwehrstrasse where they lived, along Sanderstrasse and Augustinerstrasse, halfway up Domstrasse, through the little Schustergasse to the big Green Market.

This was quite a distance for a little three and a half year old girl. It also involved crossing several cross roads with all sorts of traffic. Despite the cold, the Market was bustling with people and next thing you know, Mama and the Child became separated. Mama nearly went out of her mind looking for her little girl, shouting her name until she had no voice left.

But it was useless.The Child had vanished from the Marketplace. In despair and crying, Mama hurried to her mother's (Oma's), who lived on Domstrasse not far from the market, hoping maybe the Child had found her way there, but she wasn't there either.

Oma suggested for Mama to go home, just in case the little girl was headed there. Of course no one knew if she even knew her way home, but that's exactly what happened. When the child realized that Mama was lost, she headed straight home. Somehow, she remembered the way back. Of course when she got there, she wouldn't be able to get in because the door was locked.

Mama actually found her cold, scared and crying, but otherwise perfectly safe, just a little bit before she got all the way home. Karola remembers being hugged a lot and having her little arms and legs rubbed to warm them up and best of all, she was praised for years to come for being so smart and resourceful.

She was a lovely little girl with big brown beautiful eyes and curly dark hair, like Papa's. When she started school, she quickly became her teacher's favorite. She was sweet and well behaved eager to please and eager to learn.

Mama would walk her back home at noon. Then they would spend all afternoon practicing her letters. Every day she would fill her slate with her ABCs—no printing, but regular cursive writing, which wasn't easy for her, but it, was required homework. School was serious business, no time for fun and games.

Then Papa would come home from work and ask to see her homework. He would tell her that she did well but he was sure she could do even better, and would wipe it all off. So, she had to start all over again and it got so bad that she would start crying every time he asked to see her homework. His thinking was that "practice makes perfect" (and builds character), but Mama said that writing all afternoon was practice enough and if he wiped it off again, she would break that slate over his head. Well that was the end of that and he never erased it again.

It was quite a stretch for Mama to stand up to him like that—it definitely wasn't easy for her. She was only fifteen the first time she met him and she was instantly attracted to him and quite in awe of him. He was extremely good-looking, very worldly, always dressed nicely and just had a certain class about him. To him she was just a girl and he probably didn't even notice her.

But about three years later their paths crossed again and then one thing led to another. Mama got pregnant and Papa did the honorable thing and married her. They started their life together with absolutely nothing but their few clothes. They went and bought two plates, two forks, two knives and a pot or two.

Mama didn't even know how to cook. Papa had to teach her. Luckily he knew how. Mama had to learn a lot of things very quickly. She was just a young, dumb starry-eyed girl when she got married and Papa treated her accordingly.

Their wedding was nothing but a quick trip to the Courthouse wearing their Sunday best—in Mama's case a little black suit. She carried a little bunch of flowers Papa had bought her and he had a little gold band for her, which she ended up wearing proudly the rest of her life.

Their witness (or best man) was a friend of Papa's who treated them to dinner afterward.

They were married December 20, 1924. Four months later, on Easter Sunday morning April 12, 1925, Karola was trying to emerge.

In those days, all babies were born at home with a little help from a mid-wife. But in this case, there were complications and Papa ended up running around trying to find a doctor who would come to the house on Easter Sunday morning to deliver Karola. Obviously, it all turned out all right, but it was quite a traumatic experience for the young couple, especially Mama.

Caring for a new infant in those days was difficult to say the least. There were no conveniences then like disposable diapers, or formula, or prepared baby food. There were no shots to protect children from dreaded diseases like diphtheria, whooping cough, typhus or measles and mumps.

Needless to say, infant mortality was very high. One of the best-known and most beloved people in Wurzburg at that time was Dr. Strauss, a gifted Jewish doctor, who could just look at a patient and instantly know what was wrong. And he would treat them regardless if they could pay him or not. It was not unusual for the good doctor to give his patients a little money so they could buy medicine they needed to get better. There is no telling just how many lives—especially babies—he saved in the process.

The diseases people came down with in those days were mostly related to poverty, hard work and poor nutrition, and even poorer sanitation. People just lived in appalling conditions.

The apartment Mama and Papa rented was in a house with no electricity. They had a sink with cold running water, and the toilet was down stairs across an open balcony in a little outhouse and was shared by three other families. There were no bathing facilities at all.

Diapers had to be boiled in a big wash pot on top of the wood and coal burning stove in the kitchen, right along with dinner. The stove had a built-in water reservoir that provided hot water as long as a fire was going. The stove was also their source of heat, so it was fine in the winter, but very impractical in the summer.

Mama was really on cloud nine when they were able eventually to buy a three-burner gas stove with an oven that had a thermostat. It became one of Mama's prized possessions, because it did make her hard life a little bit easier.

One rule Papa established pretty well from the beginning was that they had to have cake on Sunday for breakfast. That was their one special treat. So every Saturday Mama had to bake a cake—nothing elaborate, just maybe a yeast cake with raisins, or a pound cake, or if fruit was cheap and plentiful, a cake bottom with fruit on top, like apples or plums. The coal stove had a baking chamber too, but it was always hard to get the heat just right. It was a whole different story cooking and baking with gas.

Gradually, in spite of Papa's low wages, they started to accumulate things. They bought a nice bedroom suite with a big three door Kleiderschrank (clothes closet) because there were no built-in closets in Germany. It was ivory colored with a little rose-colored trim and was very pretty. Along with that they bought featherbeds, because the nights get very cold in Germany. Another necessity was a Kuchenschrank (kitchen cabinet) for their increasing supply of dinner and cookware.

For transportation and recreation, they eventually bought his and her bicycles, probably from Onkel Sepp, Papa's brother who by then owned a bicycle shop in Schweinfurt. This would expand their horizon tremendously as they could travel all across the Main River valley and beyond with food and drink packed into the saddlebags on both bikes. They would leave early in the morning and not get back until night.

By then, Karola was about six or seven years old when Onkel Sepp had told her he would build a bike just for her, to which she replied, "Ich will kens" (a Wurzburger version of "I don't want one."), a phrase she hasn't lived down to this day.

Onkel Sepp was actually a master builder of racing bikes, which were used in many of the popular bike races, including the Tour de France. They were all custom-built then, tall, and light weight with very thin tires and curved handlebars. That is what Karola pictured he was going to make for her and she knew for sure that she didn't want one of those.

What Onkel Sepp actually made was a lovely three-quarter size bike with balloon tires for a nice soft ride. It was still pretty big for a seven-year old, but she mastered it pretty quickly. The hardest thing to learn was to get off, and Papa had to catch her and stop the bike.

One of their first big trips was to Tuckelhausen to visit Mama's grandma. This was about 15 to 20 miles from Wurzburg one-way and quite a distance. That was a lot of pedaling for a little girl, as she had to do one and a half revolutions with those smaller wheels to every one on a regular bike.

One thing they didn't have to worry about too much back then was traffic on the highway. Very, very few people had cars then and most traveling was done by train or bicycle, or motorcycle or on foot. People hiked great distances to get from one place to the next.

Of course, Wurzburg had a terrific streetcar system and it is still in use today. It was very economical, but it was mainly used for longer distances or when one was in a big hurry. It cost the same to go a short or long way, so it was definitely cheaper to walk a short walk.

All of this traveling ended abruptly when, to Karola's great surprise, Karin was born on December 30, 1932 at six o'clock in the evening. Nobody had prepared her for that. Actually, Mama was surprised too as Karin wasn't supposed to come until January 30. Apparently somebody miscalculated, because she was a full term baby, strong and healthy and beautiful with a thick shock of black hair.

Frau Querberitz, the mid-wife and Tante Marie, Mama's sister, were there to help Mama bring Karin into this world. Karola of course knew something was going on in Mama's bedroom; she just didn't know quite what until Tante Marie emerged from there and told her excitedly that she had a baby sister, "a real little black one," (referring to the black hair).

Well, someone had given Karola a book called "Kinder Schauen die Welt," (Children Look at the World). It had pictures and drawings and stories of children of different races from all across the world and it was absolutely fascinating stuff for someone who had never seen another race. So when Tante Marie said she had a little black sister, that's exactly what she pictured—one of those black babies from Africa in her book.

Of course, that's not how it turned out to be. And that wasn't the only disappointment. Soon Karola found out that babies demand and get lots and lots of attention and don't care who they take it away from—namely Karola. One night, Mama found her lying in bed crying her little heart out because she thought no one cared about her anymore. Of course Mama assured her that nothing could be further from the truth.

But in fact her life was never quite the same again. Instead of being "the child," she was now the big sister with all sorts of new duties and responsibilities. All the love and attention that had been showered on her had to be shared from now on. And quite possibly, Karin got the lion's share for a while, for this was the baby they could enjoy.

They were a lot more mature and relaxed by then and Karin was a really fun baby. For one thing, she never got sick and right from the start she had a healthy appetite. Mama tried her best to nurse her, but she just didn't have enough milk to satisfy this hungry baby. At thirteen days old, she started feeding Karin zwieback softened in half milk, half water and Karin loved it and thrived on it.

She was bright-eyed, and outgoing, quite curious about the world around her and quick to learn anything and everything. Her great mind, which she inherited from Papa, was quite evident right from the beginning. Most babies didn't learn to walk until they were well past their first birthday. Karin walked at eleven months. She learned by inching along Mama and Papa's newly acquired Wohnzimmerschrank and buffet, two very handsome pieces of furniture made of dark walnut with shiny inserts in the middle.

They were Papa's pride and joy, bought and paid for at great personal sacrifice. Unfortunately, they showed very clearly all the little handprints Karin left behind as she was making her way along the furniture. It was easily wiped off, but Mama didn't always have the time to go behind her with the dust rag. So Papa would come home and have a fit about the little handprints until Mama had enough and once again had to get his priorities in order. She told him that she would take the axe and hack that stuff to pieces. He must have believed her, because from then on he would wipe the prints himself and the whole thing resolved itself once Karin didn't need to hold on anymore.

But long before Karin ever started walking, Mama would put her in the baby carriage and it was Karola's job to push her up and down the street. This was quite customary and all older siblings were charged with this responsibility, as people knew how important it was for babies to get sunshine. This was really their only source of vitamin D, as nobody had thought yet of fortifying milk with it and one couldn't just buy it.

So on sunny days, Karola would be out there pushing Karin up and down the street and the same time giving Mama a little break to catch up on all the many things she had to do. Of course that got boring after a while and gradually she would venture a little bit further away from home. The Main River was not too far away and it soon became a favorite destination of Karola's.

The old Lion's Bridge, a beautiful old stone and brick bridge with two huge bronze lions guarding either end spanned the river within sight of their apartment. There was always something going on down there at the bridge and by the river. Ships were going up and down the river loaded with all sorts of freight and every ship would have a dog on it, and the people on board the ships would wave to the kids on the shore. And across the river were the hillsides covered with vineyards Wurzburg's winemaking heritage was famous for.

Then there were the wash-ships where women brought their laundry to wash in the river and that area was always a beehive of activity. There were stairs going down to the river and also to the wash-ships, as the river had been walled in to guard against flooding. It definitely was a lot more fun than walking along boring old Landwehrstrasse. But then a terrible thing happened one day.

For one reason or the other, little eight-year old Karola was sitting on the steps to the river holding a squirming baby Karin on her lap when somehow she slipped right out of Karola's arms and tumbled into the river, which was very deep at that point. Luckily, Karola was able to snatch a piece of Karin's shirt and pull her out, just before she went under. Once again she proved her resourcefulness, by taking Karin's soaking wet clothes off and laying them in the sun to dry before she took Karin back home.

Mama never realized how very close she came to losing both her little girls that day as Karola said she would not have gone home without Karin. She would have jumped in and drowned herself too because she wouldn't have been able to face Mama and Papa. It was a long time before she ever went back to the river, and the lesson she learned that day remained with her for the rest of her life—never get too close to deep water with a squirming baby, because that can sure get you into a lot of trouble.

It was probably a good thing that Mama never knew about this near tragedy as she already had so much else to worry about. The biggest problem in their lives was their financial situation. Papa never was very open with her about money. She didn't know how much he really made—he just gave her a weekly allowance for all the household expenses, a fourth of which she had to set aside each week so she could pay the rent at the end of the month. The rest just never went very far trying to feed a family of four and providing for the needs of growing children.

She balked when Papa wanted her to write down every pfennig she spent. She considered it a lack of trust on his part. She knew where the money went and that she wasn't wasting any, even if Papa accused her sometimes of not being able to manage the money. Sadly, Karola had to witness many bitter arguments and sometimes they wouldn't even speak to each other for a week or more, using Karola to relay to each other what had to be said.

It wasn't like Papa wasted the money he kept. He saved it up mark by mark to buy things like furniture and bicycles and whatever else to make their lives better. But to Mama, life would have been better if he had just given her a little more money for food and other needs. Eventually, she got a paper route, which she could do early in the morning before Papa went to work and that helped out some.

Then, when Karin was only seven or eight months old, she discovered that there was another baby on the way, which meant another mouth to feed. At first she was hoping that it wasn't true, but of course it was. She concealed it very well, as most women did back then. There were no chic maternity outfits then. Women just wore their baggiest dresses, discreetly letting out seams wherever possible. Mama was glad that all her children were born in winter and early spring because she could hide her pregnancy under her big overcoat.

It was no wonder kids didn't know where babies came from—they were told that the stork brought them and it must have sounded plausible enough since Germany had lots of storks nesting on top of people's roofs and chimneys. Traditionally, the stork would bite the mama in the leg, which is why she needed bed rest afterwards. That was their story and they stuck by it as the saying goes.

How Frau Querberitz figured into the whole scheme of things wasn't too clear but it seems like she always managed to be there when the stork made an appearance as was the case that fateful March morning when Karola's second baby sister was born. That baby of course was me and I wish I could say that it was a joyous occasion, but it wouldn't be the truth. Karola definitely wasn't thrilled about it and Mama was exhausted and worried about this new little life and all its needs.

Two

Papa took one look at me and decided that I was a "Verreckerle," in other words doomed to die. I was such a puny, pitiful little thing. Mama's body just hadn't really recovered from Karin's birth when she got pregnant again and her diet wasn't very good either. The free milk the state provided to low income expectant mothers she fed to Karin and Karola instead of drinking it herself.

Papa said the most striking thing about me were my long, spindly fingers which rested elegantly on my little chest as I was sleeping. Like Karola, I got whooping cough and double pneumonia and was plagued with ear infections, which got so bad at times that I screamed day and night because it was so painful. One time, Dr. Strauss had to make a cut behind my ear to relieve the pressure and let the infection drain out.

There were no antibiotics then or even baby aspirin. All Mama could provide was a hot or cold compress, some soothing tea, maybe some cough medicine and lots and lots of tender loving care, which she seemed to have had an abundance of. All the while, she was battling her own poor health. For several weeks she was unable to do her paper route, but she didn't want to give it up, so Tante Marie helped out and delivered the papers for her.

When Mama finally was able to resume doing it herself again, she got the shock of her life. She was told that the entire time her sister did the route, no money was turned in for the papers and they would be forced to bring charges against her, unless restitution was made immediately. Mama was flabbergasted and completely beside herself—and that's putting it mildly.

No one knows what awful calamity befell Tante Marie that would prompt her to spend money that didn't belong to her. It could have been any number of things as her financial situation was even more precarious than Mama's and her life was spent at the brink of disaster all the time.

She had a houseful of kids herself and her first ones—twins Betty and Ella—were born when she was only nineteen. One year later Karl was born and the following year Karola. Ella died after Karl was born, but then she had Rita, a frail little girl that suffered a lot from throat infections and nose bleeds. About seven years after Rita, she had Rudi and then sometime after Rudi was born she lost Rita.

I don't know, but it is quite possible that the newspaper money paid for Rita's funeral, but that is just speculation on my part. What I know for sure is that Mama wasn't going to let her sister go to jail over it. She couldn't bring herself to tell Papa about it. His opinion of her whole family wasn't that great and he definitely didn't share the love and adoration Mama had for her sister. She feared that a bombshell like that would completely destroy their relationship.

Mama approached the only person she knew that had any kind of money at all about a personal loan. He was a friend of theirs, a man with a furniture business and he had made their buffet and schrank—the very items that gave her so much grief when Karin put her fingerprints all over them. Graciously he loaned her the money and kept her secret and Mama faithfully and painstakingly paid him back, five marks at a time. It took a long time, but she paid back every pfennig she owed, but it took its toll on her. Here she had another addition to her family and at the same time a big debt to pay back that Papa knew nothing about.

She knew that there was no hope of any kind of help in this matter from Tante Marie because she never had any money or any kind of steady income. Her husband, Onkel Willie was at that time not very fond of working and when he did make some money, he enjoyed spending at least part of it in the guesthouse or the pool hall.

That is something Papa never ever did. His hobbies weren't as costly as drinking and gambling. One thing he loved to do was sing, so he joined a large choral group and at one time knew all the words to Handel's "Messiah" and a lot of other big works of that nature. He also played his guitar in a mandolin orchestra, so several days a week he would go to rehearsal after work. Then he joined a hiking club, which met on Sundays where they would hike to all different destinations and be gone all day.

By then, Karola was big enough that she could go along, which Mama greatly encouraged especially since she found out that one of the female club members was trying to get a little too friendly with Papa. There was no way Mama could go on an all day hike with two babies, but she understood that this was something Papa needed to do, after sitting all week in a smelly old shoe repair shop. But it left her sitting home alone Sunday after Sunday feeling quite lonely and humiliated. Women didn't go out without a husband on Sundays—it just wasn't done and besides, she didn't even have a decent Sunday dress to wear.

Another great passion of Papa's was dancing. He loved to go dancing and apparently he did that quite often by himself too. Probably their lowest point came one day when Mama was sick with the flu and all three of us kids were ailing and cranky and Papa came home and changed into his good clothes and his patent leather shoes and went dancing. Mama begged him not to go, but he left anyway. This was really the final straw for her.

First she cried for a while and then she made a plan. She knew about when he would be coming home and she lay there and listened for his footsteps on the cobblestone street down below. When she was fairly sure that he was approaching the house, she ran into the kitchen and opened all the gas jets and jumped back into bed and pretended to be asleep when he came in. She didn't really want to do us in, or herself, she was just so desperately unhappy and couldn't seem to make him understand. She had to get his attention somehow.

Well, he was terribly, terribly upset with her and as he turned off the gas and opened all the windows, he pointed out all the different horrible ways this could have ended. All of us kids, being so much smaller, could have died and she would have had to live with that, most likely incarcerated or who knows what else. Besides, it wouldn't have reflected on him favorably either. She was so sorry then and forever thankful that nothing happened to us. And it proved to be a turning point in their relationship too.

Things kept getting better all the time after that. He quit the hiking club and instead they would go on outings with us kids. Quite often they would be joined by Tante Marie and her gang or by other friends. German people have a passion for nature and fresh air and they're drawn to the forests, and Wurzburg has such beautiful forests and parks to walk in (I miss them greatly!).

I guess Mama got a Sunday dress for these outings. I know she got a two-seated stroller for Karin and me where we sat facing each other, but the backs went down, so we could lie down in it too when necessary. That's how they hauled us out to the woods, along with all the picnic stuff.

Sometimes Papa would even bring his portable record player, a heavy hand-cranked machine in a suitcase and records that seemed to weigh half a ton, just so we could have music with our picnic. Music was such an important part of his life. One thing he always had in his pocket was his harmonica and he could play beautifully any song one could name. He loved it all, from the heaviest classics to the simplest volksongs, of which Germany has such an abundance, and anything in between.

It is one of life's great mysteries what shaped this man, where he learned the things he knew and how he came to appreciate and value the finer things in life. He definitely didn't grow up being exposed to anything like that at all. He was born in Wurzburg on August 5, 1900, the third child of Johann and Karolina Scheller. His siblings were sister Anna, probably about seven or eight years older, and brother Josef (Onkel Sepp) about four years older.

They were a really nice solid Wurzburger family. His father was a professional soldier in the Bavarian Army, a highly respected occupation at the time. One of our proudest possessions was a huge portrait of him in his glorious uniform, spike helmet, bushy moustache and all, hanging on our wall. He was a really handsome man. Unfortunately, Papa never got to know him.

A meningitis epidemic swept the camp and he died when Papa was only two years old. One can only speculate how different things would have been if only his father had lived. Instead, his mother had a really tough struggle to raise her three children by herself. The state of Bavaria did give her some gold marks to compensate her for the loss of her husband, but it wasn't nearly enough and there definitely wasn't any money for higher education or anything of that sort, or any other kind of luxury.

Nevertheless, she was a strong-willed, hard working and very pious woman, determined to bring her children up right. Going to Mass every morning was as natural for them as getting up, and the kids practically grew up in church. Other than the priests, there was no father figure in their lives at all, not even a grandfather or uncle. At least Papa never spoke of any relatives on his father's side. That side of the family remains shrouded in mystery and I know absolutely nothing about them, not even their first names.

His grandmother on his mother's side was Anna Maria Schwartz, born sometime around 1840. She was a beautiful woman and somewhere in this world there is a portrait of her that some famous artist painted. She was kind and sweet, a widow at a young age and lived well over 90 years. When she passed away in 1932, all her children had preceded her in death including Papa's mother who had died earlier that same year. As far as I know, there were no other grandchildren besides Papa and his siblings.

There was one very vivid memory Papa sometimes talked about involving his sister. Apparently, as the girl was growing, her spine became more and more bent, probably from rickets or scoliosis, brought on by a lack of vitamins and proper nutrition. It was very painful for him to watch Anna crying as his mother and grandmother were strapping her into a heavy corset with steel rods down the back. It was a daily ritual and it must have been painful for her too and she hated it, but it was the only treatment known then. Actually, it really didn't help at all—she still ended up with a severely hunched back.

By the time Papa was in school, Anna was already working as a live-in maid and Papa rarely saw her anymore. Brother Sepp was living and being educated at a Catholic Boy's school called "The Vincentinum." So it was just Papa and his mother and she was working all the time. He would come home from school and there would be a slate with all the chores he had to do before his mother came home. He would complete each job and then wipe it off the slate, before starting his home work.

He definitely had the brains and the discipline and hunger for learning, but the German system only allowed for eight years of free schooling. To pursue a higher education one would have to go to a special school starting with fifth grade, which cost money his mother didn't have.

So at age fourteen he was out of school, looking for a master to take him on and teach him a trade. This was in 1914, the start of World War I, and times were hard and uncertain. The only job he could find was with a shoemaker, a pretty crude man that liked to drink and fight. It was not exactly a dream job, but Papa stayed with him a good two years. He had no choice, and he became a terrific shoemaker himself.

Meanwhile, his mother had met a widower with six young children, who were neglected and in dire need of a mother. He was a traveling salesman from Aschaffenburg and try as he might, it was impossible for him to do his job and also take care of all those kids. Good woman that she was, she felt that the Lord led her to marry this man and become the mother of these children in Aschaffenburg.

Papa, who never had a father in his life, acquired a stepfather at age sixteen. It was a real disaster for him. When his mother moved away from Wurzburg, he had nowhere to go when his job ended at the shoemakers. He didn't like Aschaffenburg, couldn't get along with his stepfather, didn't fit in with all those young kids and he resented how hard his mother had to work to take care of all of them, and there really wasn't any room for him at all in their crowded little apartment.

All the while, World War I was raging on. I'm not sure if he was drafted or joined on his own, but barely seventeen years old, Papa found himself in the German infantry fighting a losing war. Eventually, he was wounded and ended up in some overcrowded, understaffed make-shift hospital with rows and rows of beds full of sick and dying soldiers.

One of the most haunting and disturbing scenes he witnessed there was a guy in bed next to him, writhing and screaming for hours in horrendous agony as he was dying from tetanus. Nothing was being done at all to ease his suffering and it was a relief when, after many hours, he finally screamed his last scream.

Germany lost the war and things got really bad after that for all the German people. The Kaiser had abdicated and the newly formed Republic was floundering. Germany was paying millions of marks to England and France in war reparations. To do this, they printed more and more unsecured money that wasn't worth the paper it was printed on.

The French were occupying the Ruhrgebiet where Papa was working in the coalmines. He sometimes talked about the indignities the Germans suffered at the hands of the French soldiers, such as being hit with riding crops and chased off the sidewalks. The pay at the mines was so minimal, that six men (one of them Papa) shared a room with only three beds in it. Three would work the day shift and three the night shift and the beds practically never got cold. Along with the beds, they also shared each other's lice and parasites. It was really intolerable.

Meanwhile the economy collapsed completely. The coalmines and factories shut down and millions of people were out of work. The German mark lost all its value. Everyone was a millionaire, but it would take four billion marks to make one dollar. It took a suitcase full of money to buy a loaf of bread. People were so desperate, there was anarchy and uprisings in the streets and it was really a dangerous time.

Papa had moved back to Wurzburg and was lucky enough to find work and was able to rent a room with a bed he didn't have to share with anyone. It was during that crazy awful time that Mama was shot in the stomach. She was just a girl then, barely fifteen years old, on her way home from work, when shooting erupted in the street. Different factions were fighting for control of the government and Mama somehow got caught in the crossfire.

In spite of her wound, she made it to her front door where she collapsed in her brother's arms. She survived the bullet which was never found (there was no exit wound) but then she nearly died from thirst in the hospital because she wasn't allowed to drink anything at all. Her injuries involved her lower intestinal tract, which prompted the ban of any kind of food or drink until she was healed again.

Maybe it wasn't known then that human beings couldn't survive without water for very long. Mama just knew she was very, very thirsty. In desperation, she drank water from the roses someone had brought her to cheer her up. Then she worried that it might kill her and when it didn't, she also drank water from her roommate's flowers. Her roommate, Ludwina, was in the hospital for appendicitis that had burst, and she was very sick too. They were both about the same age and they became confidants and life-long friends.

Mama was like that, a real people person. Wherever she went, she made friends and a lot of those friendships lasted a lifetime, through all the joys and sorrows and changes that life brings. Not only was she a loyal friend, she also was extremely devoted to her family.

Her dad and mom (my Opa and Oma) were George Kemmer, born in October 1867, and Barbara Schneider, born in May 1876. They were poor country people, always working in other people's fields, never owning any land themselves. Search for a better life brought them to Frankfurt, where they were married in 1895. Their twin sons Karl and Fritz were born there in 1896.

But things must not have worked out too well there, for by the time Marie was born in 1900, they had moved back to Tuckelhausen, the village where Oma was born. Five years later, Mama was born on May 13, 1905 in Simmringen—they had apparently moved again. Then Otto, born in 1909 in Sonderhofen. Eventually, they ended up in Wurzburg, but even there they moved a lot.

Oma was a restless spirit, always searching for a better place to live and better work, but not very successful at either one of those endeavors, until she found the place on Domstrasser. Actually, it wasn't great either, but maybe she just got tired of moving. She had another set of twins, girls this time, in 1918, but they only lived a short time. Then in 1922, when she thought she was going through menopause, Hanni was born. By then, her daughter, my Tante Marie, was expecting her fourth child, Karola. Mother and daughter were expecting at the same time and the daughter delivered three months before her mother.

Mama's childhood days were spent caring for her little brother Otto and a neighbor's child. Her whole family including the older siblings would leave in the morning to work in the fields, leaving her behind to care for two toddlers. She was only five or six years old herself at the time, and this was a big responsibility for such a young child.

Otto had some kind of mental defect. The opinions were divided as to the cause of it. Some thought it was from birth, others thought it was from seizures brought on by high fevers when he was very small. German folklore has several other sayings about mentally handicapped babies, such as "the bath water was too hot when they were bathed," or "the parents were drunk when they were conceived," and various other old wives tales—all of them nonsense.

He was not mongoloid. Outwardly, he appeared completely normal and he had a pleasant, friendly easy-going personality. He just couldn't learn like other children. Today's special education classes probably would have done wonders for him, but the German school system had no such provisions or facilities and he was literally "left behind," with no schooling whatsoever.

Mama's education paralleled Papa's in duration—eight years was it. Her dream and ambition from early on was to become a professional dressmaker, to learn all the ins and outs of sewing, tailoring and pattern making. Most everything people wore back then was either made by such a person, or homemade with various degrees of skill. Mama had definite talent and great love for the profession, but her mother wouldn't hear of it. She thought more money could be made in the factory where Mama ended up working at the Frankonia Schokalade factory at age fourteen.

The little bit of money she earned had to be brought home to contribute to the family income. However Mama kept back a tiny amount of it and saved it up until she was able to fulfill at least one of her other dreams, owning a doll she had admired forever. She was in big trouble when she brought it home, but she didn't care. For the first time in her life she had a doll she could play with and cuddle and make dresses for. This love of dolls stayed with her the rest of her life.

She was a late bloomer and pretty well in the dark about human reproduction. When she had her first period at age sixteen, she didn't know what to make of it, so she asked her mother, who promptly scolded her for "pooping" in her pants. Well Mama knew better than that and went to her sister for some answers. Not that she was the best person to ask, since she came from the same background obviously.

It was the kind of ignorance that had Mama so in awe of Papa, when they first started dating. Somehow he had educated himself well beyond his eight years of schooling, mostly through reading I guess—not that he owned a lot of books. Mostly he read newspapers and periodicals and any other printed matter he could find. He would solve puzzles and chess problems and send them in and win prizes. One time his was the only correct solution to a particularly difficult problem and he won the grand prize, something like 50 marks or so.

Besides being smart, well dressed and good looking, he also had quite a romantic side to him. How in the world could a girl resist a guy who comes to her window in the evening and serenades her, which is exactly what Papa did, either by singing or playing his harmonica for her. It may seem quaint now, but young men really did that kind of thing back then and quite often it swept the girls right off their feet. Of course once they were married reality set in and things weren't so romantic anymore.

One thing Papa absolutely abhorred was moving. One of his favorite and oft-quoted sayings was "moving three times is like being burnt once." So, once they settled in Landwehrstrasse 9, that's where they stayed put.

Wurzburg is a very old town, first mentioned in the history books as a settlement between 600 to 800 AD. No, their house wasn't quite that old, but it was in the very oldest part of town, probably built sometime in the middle ages, long before people knew about electricity. Exactly when electricity was introduced to Wurzburg is not clear—apparently it was before the turn of the century though.

According to a book about old Wurzburg, the famous street car system which was previously drawn by horses, was electrified by the year 1900 and thereafter was known as the "elektrische." When power was made available to all the different neighborhoods, most people "saw the light" and jumped at the chance to have their houses electrified. But there were some, like Herr Altenhofer, our landlord, who had no use for this newfangled invention and were actually afraid of it and would not allow it in their house. Of course you can't really miss something you never had in the first place, which was true in Mama and Papa's case too.

The gas light they had in their new apartment was actually a big improvement over the kerosene lanterns Papa grew up with, and the spitting, sputtering, flickering, smelly and bad for your eyes carbide lamps Mama was used to. Each one of their four rooms had a fixture suspended from the middle of the ceiling much like an electric light fixture, except instead of a light bulb, it had a gauzy white thing called a mantle, or "Strumpf." There were chains on each side of the shade, one to open the gas pipe so the mantle could be lit, and the other to shut it off.   To light it, one would have to pull down the "on chain," light the match, hold it close to the mantle, then adjust the flow of gas with the other chain. It was definitely not as convenient as flipping a switch by the door, especially in a pitch dark room, but once lit it was comparable to electric light in brightness.

The apartment was on the third floor under the roof, which meant that all the outside walls were slanted almost from the floor to the ceiling. There were two rooms, a bedroom and a living room facing the street, and a little tiny room we called a "kammerle" and the kitchen facing the backyard. The only straight walls were the inside walls separating each room.

Mama sometimes cursed those slanted walls because they made the whole place so much smaller and made the placement of furniture extremely limited and difficult. They also lent an air of gloominess especially in the kitchen, where the one small window, flanked by massive slanted walls on each side, just could not bring in enough daylight. Of course it would have been too costly and considered extravagant to have the light on in the daytime.

The two bigger rooms were much brighter because they each had two good-sized windows together between the slanted walls. All the rooms connected to each other and there was no hallway at all. One entered through the kitchen from the landing on top of the staircase. One of the bigger rooms also had a door to this landing—a separate entrance in other words, and an elderly gentleman named Herr Herrlein who apparently had no family occupied this room.

He was an educated man, very quiet and reserved. He worked at the university and was a real book worm. He enjoyed living with this young couple and their little girl and they kind of adopted each other. But as the family grew and their possessions grew, he realized that they badly needed that other room and he found another place to live. They kept in touch with each other, though, and Mama did his laundry, mostly his shirts and linens for many years after that.

For Mama it was a chance to earn a few marks, which Herr Herrlein gladly paid, for she did a fine job not only washing and ironing his shirts, but also making repairs and replacing missing buttons. He washed his socks and underwear in his sink, so Mama didn't have to mess with that. The room he once lived in became our bedroom and the big three-door clothes closet ended up blocking the door out to the landing, as there was no other wall where it would fit.

Three

One of Mama's proud accomplishments was to have us potty trained at a very young age. It was more out of necessity than anything else, since there really was no good way to keep a diaper on a baby once the baby started crawling and toddling around. No one would have dreamed of putting safety pins on a baby, and plastic pants hadn't even been invented yet.

So as soon as we were able to sit up, Mama sat us on the potty in the morning to take care of business. Then she put us in training pants and checked on us all through the day and put us back on the potty every so often. Even at night she would wake up and put us on the potty if we were still dry. We would not even wake up. She would just hold us and go "wsh, wsh, wsh" in our little ears until there was success.

Mama was convinced that I was completely potty trained by age two. The true test came however when she decided to put Karin and me in a nearby day care center for a few hours in the morning, so she could earn a little extra money cleaning a couple of stores. It was a state-run facility, very low cost or possibly even free to low-income families, or else it would not have made sense to use it.

It may seem impossible, but I remember how utterly alone and miserable I felt, wandering around in this huge, cold yard with my pants soaking wet, surrounded by a sea of other miserable, lost little kids. I don't remember any toys, group activities, play ground equipment or anything else that might be considered fun, and I couldn't even find Karin, because they put her with a group of older children. I truly didn't know why my pants were wet or what to do about it or how to prevent it.

It was the absolute worst and most traumatic experience of my young life. Inevitably, I got very sick, got pneumonia and almost died since there were no antibiotics then. Actually, Mama had by then decided that this day-care wasn't working out too well, because there obviously was no care at all. Karin, who was older and more aware of things than I, hated going there too. So that was the end of our day care experience and much to Mama's chagrin, she had to potty train me all over again and nurse me back to health too.

Somehow she managed to hang onto her new job at the two stores. Our financial situation was just too dire to quit, plus she was still delivering the newspaper too. Since she had to leave long before Karin and I woke up in the morning, the plan was for our Oma to come right after Papa went to work and Karola left for school and take us to her house for a few hours and Mama would come by there to take us home when she was done with work—usually around 11:30 or 12:00.

This was Plan B since Plan A, the day care, didn't work out. It seemed to work much better for a while, but gradually, Oma would come later and later, sometimes not showing up until 11:00. Mama learned this from our neighbor, Frau Altenhofer, who kept an ear open for us, since she knew that we were alone.

Karin and I were blissfully unaware of time and we didn't feel alone because we had each other. We would amuse ourselves by jumping on Mama and Papa's huge German bed, playing trampoline, and learning to do forward and backward somersaults or hiding in the big soft featherbeds. Sometimes, Karin would decide that she needed to check on the fire in the kitchen stove, opening the door to the fire chamber and hacking away at the burning embers with the big fire hook, the way she watched Mama do it many times before. Sparks would be flying all over the place and I would be standing right behind her, in awe of her great courage and efficiency.

When Oma got there she would be miffed because we weren't even dressed yet and she would hurry to get us back to her place before Mama came to pick us up. After all, Mama was paying her to watch us. I don't remember ever spending a lot of time at my Oma's place, just mostly short visits and I don't really know when Mama decided to end the charade and just let us stay home by ourselves.

We didn't mind at all, we were used to it and we were locked in, so we didn't have to be afraid of intruders. We had a nice solid door with a good old fashioned lock that could only be unlocked with a key and Mama had the key. In an emergency we wouldn't have been able to get out, but we never thought about that. Thankfully it never came up. There is a saying that small children have a special guardian angel and ours must have been working overtime.

There is one other much told and retold incident from my very early childhood, but this one is slightly fuzzy in my mind. It happened in the summer of 1936. Mama and Papa had resumed their bike travels, each of them now having a bicycle seat for Karin and me. These metal seats, shaped like an oval basket cut in half, were attached right behind the handlebars and in front of the driver's eat. We sat on little pillows, and our feet rested on small brackets attached to the frame and if our little heads started nodding (which they tended to do on long trips), Papa had fastened padded boards to the handlebars for our arms and heads to rest on.

Karin always wanted to ride with Mama. So Papa would be up front with me and my baby doll, Helga in my lap. Karola would be right behind on her smaller bike and Mama would bring up the rear with Karin. Both big bikes had saddlebags hanging on each side of the rear tires, packed full of all the necessities for a happy, carefree day in the sun.

One of their favorite destinations was a place somewhat outside the city close to the river. It was some kind of picnic campground that attracted lots of people on the weekend. On that particular day, Mama and Papa had set up our picnic some distance back from the river. Nearby was a clump of shrubbery with trails on each side leading down to a broad grassy area which ended at the river. Karin and I had a wonderful time running around these bushes, she on one side and I on the other, laughing and saying "hello" as we met at each end and just doing this over and over, totally absorbed in this fun game.

But then someone started intruding in this game. I seem to remember a man and a woman sitting on a blanket near the end of that trail in the grassy area by the river. They would call to me as I was running by there on my way back up the other side of the trail and sometimes they would pretend like they were going to catch me and I seem to remember some candy being offered. And that's pretty well the extent of my memory.

I don't really know who first noticed that I hadn't come back up that trail. But once it was established that I had disappeared, everybody out there started asking for me, searching every inch of that campground. A lot of people had been sitting along the banks of the river and nobody had seen a child fall in, so that was ruled out.

In the midst of all this commotion and excitement a woman arrived from town and was asking what was going on. When told that a little child had vanished, she said that she had seen a man walking toward town with a crying child in his arms. She even stopped him and asked why the child was crying and he gave some evasive answer.

Well, Papa got on his bike and pedaled toward town as fast as he could and caught up with the man and me. I was crying because I wanted my Mama and I knew he was up to no good because he said he was taking me to her but I knew where she was and that he was walking further and further away from her. This much I do remember however there was no woman with him so that part could be wrong.

Anyway, Papa confronted him, asked him what the big idea was of taking his child. His lame excuse was that he thought I was lost and he was taking me to the police station. There was no way to prove otherwise and Papa just had to let him go. It is up to anybody's imagination what this person's true intentions were, but I would just as soon not even think about it.

We never ever went back to that place again, but that doesn't mean that our Sunday excursions ended. We just avoided such crowded, popular areas and headed more and more into the woods. The "Gutenberger Wald" near Wurzburg, a huge, beautiful peaceful forest, soon became a big favorite of ours, along with our brand new possession—a hammock.

First order of the day would be to find a suitable spot with two properly spaced trees. Then Papa would string up the hammock high off the ground and put Karin and me in it, safely tucked away while the rest of the camp was set up. We couldn't get down even if we wanted to, it was so high up, but we didn't want to anyway.

It was sheer heaven to be lying in this hammock, gently swaying in the breeze, looking up at the tall trees that seemed to touch the sky. Papa would join us in the hammock and play his harmonica while Mama and Karola got the food ready. It almost always was potato salad and breaded pork chops that Mama had cooked the night before and we had sweet, cold peppermint tea, and some of our Sunday cake. It all tasted wonderful out in the clean fresh air.

After dinner, it was Mama's turn in the hammock, and Karola would take us exploring, not too far off of course. We would pick wildflowers and collect pinecones and Karola loved to chase little frogs and salamanders. She wasn't even afraid to touch them and sometimes she would bring a box to take them home in. She really was still a little girl herself, but to Karin and me she seemed more like a grown up.

The poor girl got stuck a lot with taking care of us. Other than school, she rarely got to go anywhere alone. She either had to take us along or not go at all. Mama did allow her to have friends over and she had one friend,

Hildegard Spiegel, who loved coming over. She had no siblings herself, so she got a big kick out of Karola's little sisters.

She taught us lots of songs—little children's songs—that sounded so cute when children sang them. And the girls played games with us and read to us, but they actually didn't have much time doing bigger girls things together. In hindsight, I really feel sorry about that. Eventually, Hildegard's family moved away and we really missed her for a long time afterwards.

If having to baby-sit siblings all the time makes one miserable, Karola had lots of company right across the hall from us. The family that shared the third floor with us was the "young" Altenhofers, a family with six children. Their oldest, a son named Ludwig (Lulu for short) was somewhat younger than Karola, and he also spent his childhood watching his little brothers and sisters.

He didn't even get to be the only child for as long as Karola did—well maybe four or five years. Then they had Max, and after him Else, who was the same age as Karin, then Annie who was six days older than me. Exactly one year to the day later, Karlemann was born (he and Annie shared the same birthday). Right after Karlemann was Georg.

Mama said it was a sight to behold when Lulu and Karola took us to the park—the "Glasis." Lulu would have Georg and Karlemann in the buggy and the rest hanging onto the buggy and Karola, of course, would have the two of us. Wisely enough they stayed away from the river. The Glacis was actually in the opposite direction, but they did have to cross busy Sanderstrasse to get to it.

They took us there a lot, just to get us out of the house. There really wasn't a lot to do there. There were no play grounds then at all and it was forbidden to step on the grass, so we had to be mindful to stay on the sandy walkways. There was one big sandy area with park benches all around and a big water fountain in the center where we could drink if we got thirsty. That is usually where we played chase or hide-and-seek or we would draw patterns in the sand with a stick and play hopscotch or marbles and we would bring a ball sometimes. Sometimes other kids would join us there and we would form big circles and play different games that way.

Meanwhile our Mamas would be at home hard at work cleaning, washing, cooking, baking sewing and whatever else, as everything had to be done by hand and from scratch. Machines to make life a little easier hadn't been invented yet or if they were, people couldn't afford them, or in our case didn't have electricity to run them.

Oddly enough, the young Altenhofers who lived on the same floor with us and shared the same dark staircase with us, had electricity, only because they lived in the "ell," a right-angled addition to the main house that jutted into the backyard. The "old" Altenhofers who lived directly below us owned the house and didn't allow electricity in their house, but the young son, our neighbor, insisted on having it put in his apartment.

The addition had a flat roof, with no attic and one could actually walk around on it. There was an access door to it from our attic. The flat roof meant that there were no dormers or slanted walls at all in their three big rooms, just straight walls and big windows with beautiful drapes. It was really a bright, friendly place.

Something always smelled good over there too. To feed all those children, Frau Altenhofer was cooking and baking things all the time and she was generous—always trying to give us little tastes of things, which we were quite often too shy to accept. She was a spunky little woman (think Dr. Ruth Westheimer) real outgoing and always laughing.

We suspect that Mama learned some of her spunk over there, as the two women often sat together in the evening after all the kids were in bed. Mama would bring her sewing basket that was always full of things that needed mending and repairing. Frau Altenhofer did finishing work for a furrier, putting silk lining in fancy fur coats, all done by hand—really painstaking work—quite often under pressure to have it done by a certain date.

But they had fun with it too. They would try on these really expensive coats and feel very rich for a few minutes. A big fashion statement back then was to wear the pelt of a fox or a weasel around one's shoulder, complete with heads, feet and tail. Frau Altenhofer lined these too in silk. She would have them lying on her table while she was working on them and they were a startling sight with their beady little eyes. She sewed a little clip to their mouth so they could "bite" their tail and that was how they were worn around the shoulder.

They would have the radio softly playing "request parade" with all the popular performers and hit songs from that era. Of course, that's another thing we couldn't have without electricity—a radio. We were just hopelessly old fashioned, while everything over there seemed very modern—like stepping from the nineteenth century to the twentieth century just by crossing the hall.

But there was a dark side to this. The Altenhofer's was a very volatile relationship, stemming at least partially from the fact that she was Lutheran and he was Catholic. The children were raised in their mother's faith, which apparently didn't sit too well with Herr Altenhofer. Normally he was very quiet and soft spoken, but when he got drunk he turned into a completely different person and he did this usually on the kid's special days, such as Lulu's confirmation.

One of a child's first big events in their life is their First Communion or when they are confirmed. The Catholics have it in third grade, the Lutherans in seventh and it is a big family celebration, much like a small wedding with lots of flowers and decorations and a big feast with all the relatives—just a very special occasion. In this case, Herr Altenhofer chose not to attend his son's confirmation, and he was absent at the celebration afterwards too.

But Frau Altenhofer came from a very large, close-knit family. She had at least three sisters and several brothers, and the sweetest little mother, Frau Dehler. They all gathered around to celebrate Lulu's day. The fun and merriment lasted well into the evening. My bed was right next to the wall next to the hallway and I could hear them talking and laughing and having a gay old time and then the very noisy good-byes as all the guests were leaving.

For a few minutes it was fairly quiet over there and then there were more footsteps on the stairs (they were wooden, old and creaky and very loud). This was Herr Altenhofer coming home, very drunk. Next thing you know, there was terrible screaming and yelling and loud weeping and dishes being smashed—the most frightening, distressing sounds I had ever heard.

This was the first time I heard it, but it wasn't the last. It actually became a fairly regular occurrence. Most of their holidays were ruined that way and I felt so sorry for them. But they all acted like nothing happened afterwards, acting quite superior sometimes, and Frau Altenhofer always laughing and being very cheerful and happy. No doubt she loved her children very much and tried to shield them as much as possible, especially the girls, and this was their way of coping with this heartache and embarrassment.

Two of Frau Altenhofer's sisters were married, well off and childless. One lived in Nurnburg, the other in Schweinfurt. The one in Nurnburg, a good distance from Wurzburg, really loved Else and wanted to raise her, which they ended up doing. They had a house and a car and even a dog—things only wealthy people had—and so Else had a much better life than her siblings, but she became estranged and "stuck up" and really lost that closeness with them.

Annie often visited the aunt in Schweinfurt and probably could have stayed there, but she got homesick and missed her family very quickly and never stayed very long. She loved her brothers and, not surprisingly, was quite a tomboy herself, not at all into dolls, or playing with dollhouses the way Karin and I did. But we were buddies anyway. She would come over, sometimes half heartedly bringing her one and only doll with her, but we usually ended up playing other games with her.

One game Lulu liked to play with me and Annie was "brides." He was very much into decorating and beautifying his world and the people in it. He would drape us with old lace curtains or tablecloths and make wreaths out of flowers for our hair and set up an altar with candlesticks for the wedding. He was the wedding director, but the trouble was we had no grooms, because Karlemann and Georg were just little boys and they didn't want to cooperate.

It was hard to think of them as bride grooms anyway since most every time I went there they were sitting on their respective potties, looking at picture books and taking care of business. Or they were rolling around the floor wrestling with each other. We always knew when it was naptime over there because Georg was a rocker.

Even though the children's bedroom was at the far end of the "ell," after the kitchen and the master bedroom, we could hear him banging his crib against the other beds as he was rocking himself to sleep. No one could stop him from doing this. The whole room was, of course, mostly beds for all those kids. At night they would put him to bed first and wait until he was done rocking and asleep before they all went to bed. Sometimes it took a long time.

Their financial situation was somewhat better than ours. Herr Altenhofer was a gardener by trade, working for the city, plus he and his parents leased a large tract of land where they grew all kinds of vegetables, flowers, and fruit trees. It was a thriving business, seasonal of course, starting early in the spring and lasting well into the fall. In the heights of summer they were so busy that everybody had to pitch in.

But they were able to send Lulu to "oberschule" in preparation for college. Annie went to ballet school for a while which was connected to the theater. She was small and cute and very agile and not at all shy or self-conscious. Everybody was very proud of her when she was selected to play Madam Butterfly's child on stage—a little boy actually. We didn't get to see her though because children weren't allowed, but I believe Mama went.

Children weren't allowed in movies either, unless it was some fairy tale made especially for children, with real people, not cartoons, and only in the mornings. I still remember the very first movie I ever saw. It was "Frau Holle" straight out of my Grimm's Fairytale book and it was such a special occasion for Karin and me that we wore our Sunday best even though it wasn't Sunday.

Most likely it was Karin's first movie too because we did everything together. She sometimes thought that it was unfair that I got to do everything she got to do, since I was so much younger, and she was probably right. She had no special privileges for being older, but if we did something stupid and got in trouble, she got most of the blame because "she was older and should have known better" (Mama's words).

To be perfectly honest, I was no "goody two shoes" myself, but she was more daring, more inquisitive, more mischievous, more outgoing and that's what made her such a fun sister. She was also more prone to break things and of course, it was never her fault. Stuff just happened to her and she would always say, "nix dazn gekount" (it wasn't her doing), a phrase that stuck with her all her life. Whenever something broke, that's what we said, even Papa liked to tease her with that phrase.

It really was quite amazing, the transformation Papa underwent in just a few short years. Where Karola mostly remembers him as the stern disciplinarian of her young age, Karin and my memories of him are more of a fun-loving, playful, affectionate nature, who left the disciplining completely up to Mama. That doesn't mean, however, that we didn't respect him, we had tremendous respect for him and wouldn't have dreamed of disobeying him in any way, but it was out of love, not fear.

One thing he loved to do was to scoop us up, cradle us in his arms and swing us back and forth. We called it "schaukeln" and we couldn't get enough of it. Or he would come home on payday evening probably on a Saturday, clutching his little briefcase to his chest, proceeding to pull out little bags filled with goodies and holding them up high for us to see. Our eyes would get bigger and bigger at all these treasures and it took us years to figure out that he was actually showing us the same little bag over and over. His favorite store for these treats was the "Spanish garden" on Augustinerstrasse, a store that specialized in fine imported wines and fruits and also all sorts of chocolates. It smelled absolutely heavenly in there from all those exotic things.

Four

Papa loved to introduce us to new things like dried figs and dates or wonderful blood oranges, which had red streaks inside and were incredibly sweet and juicy and none of these things grew in Germany at all. And we would get a piece of chocolate on Sunday morning in bed before we got up. We had to stay in bed until Mama or Papa got up and started the fire in the kitchen stove to warm up the kitchen. It would get bitter cold in there overnight because Papa was a big believer in fresh air and we always slept with the window open.

During the week the only warm place we had was our little kitchen, the other rooms were dark and icy cold and we would just dash through them to jump into bed, which we warmed up with a big round metal hot water bottle. But on Sunday afternoon, if the weather was too bad to go anywhere they would light a fire in the potbellied stove in the living room and Papa would crank up the record player and dance around the room with us with our feet on top of his. Or he would gently guide Mama in a slow waltz. That was her favorite.

We had a really nice selection of records, not huge, but enough for a Sunday afternoon without repeating any. They were the old 78's that could only be played one at the time and the record player had to be cranked up between each record. To this day, the music on those records is etched into my brain and if I happen to hear one, it brings all those memories flooding back. Karin was exactly the same way and certain times will forever be connected to those lovely Sunday afternoons.

In the evening, as the sun went down and the room slowly turned dark, nobody would rush to light the gaslight. First we would have "Dammerstundchen" (the hour of dusk). We would all pile together around Papa on the sofa, where he would be strumming his guitar and we would sing along and watch the flames through the cracks in the stove making patterns on the ceiling and walls. If this seems like it would be terribly boring for children, it really wasn't. We actually treasured those fleeting moments of closeness and togetherness when Mama and Papa were relaxed and happy and not hard at work, as they were all through the week. It was extremely rare to ever see either one of them doing absolutely nothing, it just didn't happen.

Papa was forever repairing all the relatives' and neighbors' shoes in our kitchen to earn a little extra spending money. He had a long narrow low workbench right under the slanted wall by the window that held all his shoemaker tools and equipment. There were all sorts of hammers, very sharp special knives, awls to punch holes in the leather, and special yarn that he strengthened with beeswax to sew the soles to the tops. He had wooden nails and metal ones and a big iron plate, shaped to fit over his legs, with a hole in the middle that held all the different size iron feet upside down, over which the shoes were slipped to work on the bottoms. There were also wooden feet of different sizes that were adjustable to different widths.

It was all fascinating stuff and Karin and I liked to mess with it sometimes, even though that was a big no-no (I guess we did disobey sometimes!). Mama sometimes complained about all these smelly old shoes in our kitchen, but it was just something we had to live with. Papa never ran out of work, because the long distances people walked were hard on their shoes and the cobblestone streets were murder on high heels.

Even then, ladies liked to be stylish. We used to laugh about Frau Altenhofer's high heels that Papa repaired time and time again. She was short and overweight with big, wide feet, which she would squeeze into these elegant little high-heeled pumps and completely squeeze them out of shape.

Papa, who had a very fitting saying for every situation, would say "country bumpkin feet in Parisian shoes." Paris was back then the epitome of elegance and style, of course, and probably is to this day. Mama didn't go for style, so she wore sensible shoes. But when our cousins Betty and Karola started wearing heels, theirs also often ended up on Papa's workbench and Karin and I loved to clomp around in them—another no-no.

When he wasn't working on shoes, he was busy creating wondrous things for us out of cigar boxes, which were made of wood back then, and free for the taking. He couldn't afford to smoke cigars or even pre-made cigarettes so he just bought tobacco and papers and rolled his own. It was actually fascinating to watch him roll up a whole batch, enough to fill his neat little cigarette case he always carried with him.

Somehow he must have suspected that smoking wasn't the healthiest thing for him to do, so he used a cigarette holder with a filter inside, which turned really brown and yucky after a few days and needed to be changed a lot. This gave him a false sense of security, if not smugness, thinking that all the bad stuff stayed in the filter instead of his lungs. Nicotine is a very powerful addiction and it definitely had Papa in its grip.

Other than the smoking, he was actually very health conscious and way ahead of his time where food was concerned. He knew about vitamins long before anyone else talked about them. He knew that potatoes and vegetables were loaded with all sorts of nutrients and therefore good to eat, but they couldn't be boiled in too much water as that leached out all the vitamins.

Too much cooking also destroys the vitamins, so they bought something like a pressure cooker with two inserts that had holes in them. The meat went on the bottom and when it was almost done, the potatoes were added in the first insert. After they were almost done, the green beans or whatever was added in the second insert on top. Everything was steamed to perfection in a short time with all the vitamins intact, since no water touched the potatoes or vegetables.

For added nutrition and flavor, Mama added fresh chopped chives and parsley, which she grew in pots on the windowsill, and she added these to just about everything we ate. That tasted fine in most things, but I sure didn't care for the chives in cottage cheese, which we ate with boiled potatoes.

Actually we ate everything with boiled in the jacket potatoes, because they were the mainstay of our diet. Every fall we had 400 to 500 pounds delivered directly from a farmer in one of the surrounding villages. They were brought to town in a wagon drawn by oxen or cows and stored in our lockable little cubicle in the basement, where Papa had built an ingenious box with a slanted bottom and an opening near the bottom. This enabled us to get to the bottom of the pile and prevented rotting.

After all, that's what got us through the winter and had to last until the new potatoes were ready in the spring or summer. Every evening, without fail, we boiled a pot of potatoes to eat with either the cottage cheese (with chives) or limburger cheese that smelled to high heaven, or blood sausage with lots of gristle in it, or "buckling" which were smoked fish with needle sharp bones in them.

Our big meal was eaten at noon or midday. In the winter, when very few fresh vegetables were available, it mostly consisted of thick soups, such as split pea or dried beans with little sausages, or lentil soup with dumplings, which we loved. When we had potato soup, we always had hot cocoa and freshly baked sweet rolls from the bakery afterwards—one tradition we didn't mind at all.

On Sundays, we had a small pork roast with potato balls or mashed potatoes and either red cabbage or Brussels sprouts, which was all that was available in winter. We also had red beets and celery knobs, which Mama boiled and pickled and that was our salad. It got a little monotonous during the long winter months and we really welcomed spring and all the "firsts" it brought—first fresh green salad, cucumbers, spinach, peas, new potatoes, and carrots. They all tasted so wonderful after not having had them all winter.

Without refrigeration, shopping for milk and other perishable things was pretty well a daily necessity. We boiled the milk to improve its taste and extend its lifespan somewhat, but on long, warm summer weekends when we bought a little extra because stores were closed on weekends, it often turned sour. Of course, nothing was ever thrown away. We just left the sour milk in a warm place until it turned thick and clabbered and then ate it with rye bread. It tasted a lot like plain, unflavored yogurt and Mama really loved it, but we weren't too crazy about it and had to eat it anyway.

One time the sour milk got a little bit past the clabbered stage, so Mama decided to try and turn it into pot cheese by leaving it sitting in the sunny living room window in a covered dish. I guess the warmth was supposed to speed up the aging process. It turned into the foulest smelling, most awful yellowish-brown mess, ten times worse than limburger cheese, but Mama wanted us to try it anyway. Karola and Karin flatly refused, so she turned to me with a whole spoonful of that stuff, but the stench made me gag and she gagged right along with me. This was one experiment that "went sour" and she never tried to make pot cheese again.

One way to keep things kind of cool was to set them outside the kitchen window overnight, where Papa had enlarged the outside windowsill and put a little railing around it for that purpose. But there was a problem with that too of course. Since plastic wrap, aluminum foil, zip lock bags or Tupperware with tight fitting lids had not been invented yet, there was no adequate way to protect anything properly from whatever critters were lurking about out there—mainly flies, birds, mice or cats. The cats were mostly kept to chase the mice away, but they didn't always do such a great job.

One time Mama even thought we had rats, which leads me to the mystery of the missing pork chops. Mama had fixed extras for next day's dinner or whatever, but when she was ready to use them, they had disappeared. They had been stored on a shelf in a cabinet that had a curtain in front of it, on a plate, but now the plate was empty. At first, accusing fingers were pointed at each other, but everyone's conscience was clear. Nobody had eaten the pork chops. Certainly not Karin and I because we were still babies then and Karola hadn't done it either.

It was totally baffling and very strange, and it remained unsolved for quite some time, until one day Mama decided to move the cabinet. There she discovered a hole in the wall close to the floor and in front of the hole were her pork chop bones, which were too big to fit through the hole. Mama swore it had to be rats to carry off such big pork chops, but Papa said the hole was too small for rats. In any case, he wanted to make sure nothing would ever come through there again, so he broke several beer bottles and put the glass shards in the hole before sealing it with gypsum. They were amazed how many broken beer bottles this hole held, but they felt really good about having stopped this invasion once and for all.

Sometime after that, Mama heard the landlady, the old Frau Altenhofer complain that someone had thrown a bunch of broken beer bottles in the bathroom down below us. This so called bathroom was actually no more than a little cubicle with a toilet that had the tank high up near the ceiling with a long chain attached for flushing and there were two such cubicles—one for all the people upstairs, and one for downstairs, which we weren't allowed to use except in a real emergency. We didn't like to use that one anyway because it had a big hole in the ceiling that nobody ever bothered to repair and that explains how our broken bottles ended up in that bathroom.

Even though these bathrooms were inaccessible from the house, one had to walk across a balcony in front of Frau Altenhofer's kitchen window to get to them. They were covered by the same roof, as was the balcony and they shared the same end wall and that's how these rats or mice got into our kitchen. One would think that an old house like that, with walls made out of plaster of Paris with straw inside and lots of cracks all over, would be infested with all sorts of vermin, but that's not true at all. I never saw cockroaches (German or otherwise) until I came to America, believe it or not.

The nasty little pests we did have were tiny red bedbugs and Mama hated them with a passion. Out of all the family, they loved me best of all and they really tormented me with itchy bites, which turned into ugly sores because I scratched them with dirty fingernails. Mama was forever tearing all the beds apart, checking all the seams and piping on the mattresses because that's where these little bedbugs liked to hide out.

She would pierce them with a long needle, scooping up a whole string of them and then squash them all at once. Then she sprayed every thing down with her "Flit" pump sprayer. She would have this really sick look on her face, knowing that she was fighting a losing battle and before long she would have to do it all over again.

Whenever she changed the bed linens she inspected all the mattresses, which about every six to eight weeks when we had a date at the "waschkuche." It would have been impossible to wash such big items in our little kitchen and the wash-kitchen down below, which was there for all the tenants to use, was actually useless because the big wash kettle had a big crack in it. Luckily there was a place called a Miele waschkuche where for a few marks, one could wash to one's heart's content and all the equipment was in working order. It was a busy place and appointments had to be made well in advance and kept at all cost. And what a big operation it was!

First of all, we had to borrow our Opa's "leiterwagen," a four-wheeled wooden wagon with ladder-like sides and wooden spoke wheels with metal rims around them. It was an indispensable item in those days. Everything that was too heavy to carry, such as hundred pound sacks of coal, or potatoes, or briquettes, or loads of wood for kindling, or in our case, huge wicker baskets full of dirty laundry was hauled in these wagons—and sometimes even kids. Karin and I loved to ride in it, even though these wooden wheels clattered on the cobblestone streets and rattled our bones and teeth, Mama and Karola would pull us home.

Then we would load up the two big baskets, an oval one and a rectangular one, and haul them to the washing place. This was the night before the big washday. Nothing was ever washed unless it really needed it—in other words was good and dirty. So, everything had to be soaked overnight in big tubs filled with water and washing soda. Early the next morning when we went back over there, the proprietor would already have the big wash kettle fired up ready for the soap powder and the linens, which had to be squeezed through a manually operated wringer to get rid of the dirty soaking water.

All the white linens had to be boiled for a while, and then spread out on the big tables and the dirtiest areas attacked with lye soap and scrub brushes. Everything else was washed in a similar manner except for the boiling. Once everything was thoroughly scrubbed, it had to be rinsed at least twice in clear water to get all the soap out. It was back breaking work for Mama and we kids couldn't really be of any help, except to stay out of the way, as it was a pretty dangerous place to be.

Oma came whenever she could to help and wash some of her things at the same time. Tante Marie was only too glad to bring her dirty laundry when she found out that we had a date at the washkuche, but rarely showed up to help. Mama did a lot for her sister and never expected (or got) much in return. Washing was very hard work, without any kind of machines and then there was another huge problem of how to get all these big items dry.

In summer, when the weather was nice, we hauled it to the "talavera," which was a huge meadow by the Main River, covered with public clotheslines for anyone's use. It was a pretty good distance to walk, from where we lived, but it was a beautiful spot, sunny a breezy and it seemed like fun at first. But as the day wore on, it got pretty boring, watching the laundry dry. Mama would run some errands and just leave us there with Karola to watch so no one would run off with our stuff.

We did enjoy playing hide and seek between all those big sheets, but we had to be really careful not to touch them with our dirty little hands, or Mama would get really upset. And then there were the geese that stayed down there, a large flock of them, and they didn't like kids at all. We tried to stay away from them as far as possible, but they would find us and chase us with their necks stretched straight out and hissing like snakes. They were nasty!

After everything was finally dry, we had another date to keep, this one at the pressing place. Everything was made out of 100% cotton, and wrinkled very badly. It would have taken many hours to iron all those big sheets and featherbed covers and pillowcases, and tablecloths.

We just had two little flat irons, which we headed on the stove, with one heating while the other was being used. Sometimes they would get to hot and singe whatever was touched with them. Mama never owned an ironing board; she just put a blanket on the kitchen table and covered it with an old sheet. That's how she ironed. She had a sleeve board, to iron the little poofy sleeves and things.

In summer we hauled all the big flat pieces to this place that had huge electric hot roller presses. One would feed all these wrinkled things in on one side and out came beautifully smooth linens on the other side. It was amazing and quick and left a wonderful, fresh, clean smell behind. We liked going there.

Winter with its five months of cold, wet weather was quite a different story. To dry laundry outdoors was impossible then, so we hauled it from the washkuche straight up to the attic above our apartment where Papa had strung wire. There it would hang, alternately freezing and thawing out and freezing again overnight.

By the time it was finally dry, it often had soot on it because the red tile roof was not all that airtight and everybody's chimney was puffing clouds of black smoke all over the place. Mama would just bring down a few pieces at a time and iron them on the kitchen table, often fussing about the soot or the smudges the irons left behind from sitting on the stove.

When she wasn't busy with that or all the other things she had to do, she would be sewing. I vaguely remember when she first got her treadle-sewing machine. It was a real "red letter day" for Mama. She was so proud and happy. And from then on, everything we three girls wore Mama created with her two hands. What we wore before that is anybody's guess, because ready-made clothing was not readily available yet. Mass production of clothing came later.

Of course, everything Mama made for Karin, she also made for me, except it was a little smaller. She was a strong believer in complete equality and people often mistook us for twins. Karola's style was different from ours, after all she was a budding young lady by then, but she would get something similar in material.

Mama was proud of her handiwork, as she should have been. After all, she didn't get to learn how to sew, she just taught herself and figured it out on her own. Her patterns and ideas she got from a monthly women's magazine to which she subscribed and which she also delivered all over town on her bicycle to other subscribers. She delivered several other magazines that way too.

The patterns in her magazine were actually just one big sheet of paper with lots of differently printed lines on both sides. This would be pinned to some brown paper and certain striped or dotted, or otherwise marked lines were followed with a sharply spiked metal wheel, which made little holes in the brown paper underneath, leaving an outline which could then be cut out and there would be a pattern. This actually became Karin's and my job as we got older and we loved doing it. Ours were such simple pleasures.

Five

I still remember how excited everybody was when the Zeppelin came to Wurzburg. It was rare to even see an airplane then, much less one of those huge airships. No one had ever seen one in person. And it came on a holiday no less, so everybody had ample time to go and admire it. It was supposed to be tethered at Wurzburg's airfield (the flugplatz) up on the hill for a few hours.

Of course we had to go see it—wild horses couldn't have kept us away. We could have just walked straight up the hill, but it was quite a distance and the road was too steep for the bikes, so Papa decided to approach the field from behind, where the roads weren't nearly as steep. But we got lost somehow and it had rained a lot and we ended up on some terribly muddy dirt road where the bikes got completely bogged down. Everybody had to get off and slosh through the mud, and then it started raining some more. By the time we found the airfield, it was coming down in buckets and we got soaked to the skin.

I don't know if the Zeppelin was still there or not. I never saw it. They just put us back on the bikes and took the shortest route home—straight down that steep hill. The trip wasn't a total loss though because that muddy dirt road was lined with apple trees and the storm had knocked down lots of apples. They were just lying there waiting to be picked up and we proceeded to fill up the saddlebags on the bikes. Although still slightly green, Mama turned them into delicious applesauce, which was a rare treat for us and it was free! My best guess is that this was the fall of 1937.

It was in the coldest part of winter, probably January, when Tante Anna, Papa's sister disappeared. Her life had actually dramatically changed for the better. The family whom she had worked for and served faithfully for many years had included her in their will and when they passed away, left her with a tidy little inheritance. She wasn't rich by any means, but she was comfortable with a nice place of her own and a much better life. And she even had a boyfriend, a man who worked at the justice department. It is pretty safe to assume that she had met him there while settling her affairs regarding the inheritance.

Life at last was good for Anna and no one deserved it more, but it was short-lived. One day she simply vanished. Then a woman came forward to tell of a couple she had observed strolling along the river's edge. It was a bitter cold, gloomy and slightly foggy winter evening, not at all conducive to a leisurely stroll and that is what caught her attention. Most people avoided being out at all in that kind of weather and at that time of day, or they hurried to their destinations.

What totally shocked her was what quickly followed next. The two people began to struggle with each other and the woman, who appeared to have a hunched back, was pushed into the icy cold Main River where her heavy winter clothes pulled her straight down to the bottom. She never came back up, probably didn't even know how to swim. When this sad story came to light, it became pretty clear that this brutally murdered woman most likely was Papa's sister Anna.

The boyfriend was investigated and he freely admitted having been at the river with her in her last moments of life. But he said she was suicidal and the struggle the woman had seen was actually his heroic effort at trying to prevent her from jumping. He was so terribly distraught over her death and his failure to save her that he had a nervous breakdown and that's why he hadn't reported it. Apparently all his friends at the justice department believed him and he got away with it. And it wasn't long before he produced a will signed by Anna leaving all her money and worldly possessions to him.

It was a sad day and probably one of the worst things Papa ever had to do, when her body was finally found and he, as the next of kin, had to go to the morgue and identify it. Even though she had been in the river a long time, the icy water had preserved her enough to be recognizable and it was indeed his sister Anna and that was all he would say about it. There had to be a funeral, but I have no memory of it at all, so I can't write about that. I do remember visiting her grave once in a while, especially on All Saints Day, November 1st, when traditionally people put candles and flowers on their loved one's graves.

It has been said that bad things happen in bunches and when it rains it pours. But it was totally unexpected when in the summer of 1938 Mama gave birth to a dead little baby boy. She was in her sixth month of a completely normal pregnancy when she went into spontaneous premature labor after carrying a heavy basket of laundry upstairs. When she realized what was happening, she sent Karola to get help, but the baby was born before anybody could get there.

It was a beautiful, completely formed tiny baby right down to its tiny little finger and toe nails, just about the size of my beloved baby doll Helga. But it was blue and it never drew a breath and most likely it was dead even before Mama carried that basket upstairs. Since it never actually lived, it never was baptized, never had a name and didn't have a Christian burial. It was just considered a specimen.

Mama and Papa placed it in a shoebox and Papa took it to the "anatomie," a place where they studied and preserved specimens. But Mama grieved for that little boy, she wanted so much to give Papa a son and she had bonded with that baby while it was growing inside her. I'm sure Papa was sad too, but he never talked much about his feelings.

Actually, his feelings were not the upper-most thing on his mind at that particular time. It was his body that was giving out on him, making him suffer from excruciating pain in all his joints. All those years of sitting on a stool, hammering away at people's shoes, doing essentially the same movements over and over, day in and day out were at last catching up with him. Even his so-called leisure time activities consisted of much the same movements as he was nailing and gluing old boards together making dollhouses for us.

With only the crudest of tools and infinite patience, he created all the furniture for them out of cigar boxes and then painted it all, mostly at night after we went to bed. One Christmas, he surprised us with a fully functioning Ferris wheel, also made of cigar boxes, for our little doll house dolls with beautifully shaped gondolas and a carousel with little seats suspended by chains. The middle part of it was made of empty spools of thread. Both had cranks to make them turn, and out of scraps and discards he created the most wonderful toys that we enjoyed playing with for many years. But it all involved sitting and using his right arm. And then he just couldn't do it anymore, he was in so much pain that he couldn't lift a hammer or sit on a stool.

It must have seemed like the end of the world to Papa when Dr. Strauss told him bluntly, "Christian, you have to find a different job!" One of Dr. Strauss' most endearing qualities was that he didn't mince words and that he called everyone "du" and by their first names. He didn't believe in all that stiff formality of calling each other "sie," and "Mr.," or Mrs.," so-and-so, which is still done to this day in Germany.

Of course we didn't know it then, but it was really a blessing in disguise, bordering on divine intervention when Papa couldn't work as a shoemaker anymore. He applied at and was hired by the German railroad, which is government owned and run, and he started there in August of 1938. Without any particular skills or education, he had to start at the very bottom as a common laborer and the work was hard and dirty with long hours.

Sometimes he would be gone for days because he was part of a team that had to clear the rubble whenever there was a train wreck, sometimes a long distance away. He saw some pretty gruesome sights sometimes and he really dreaded that part of the job. But at the same time, all his physical ailments were going away and all that exercise and hard work were actually making him stronger and feel better. The money was better too and so were the benefits and now we even had health insurance, something we never could afford before.

This was a very good thing, because Dr. Strauss, the "savior" of the poor people of Wurzburg, who never pressured anyone for payment for his services and quite often even "forgot" to send a bill, was getting ready to leave Germany forever. It was actually forbidden to go and see him or associate with him in any way because he was Jewish, and it could have dire consequences if one was caught or even suspected of doing so.

In spite of the danger we went to see him one last time to say good-bye. I remember Mama looking carefully up and down the street before entering the house where he lived and had his office. It was hard getting down his hallway as there were huge crates sitting everywhere filled with all the latest medical equipment, x-ray machines, and all of his furniture of course. Apparently there was a limit on the actual cash money that could be taken out of the country, but not on personal possessions, so Dr. Strauss made the most of it. He was headed for Amerika for a whole new fresh start on life.

Many years later, we found out that he ended up doing exactly what he had done so well in Germany, which was taking care of and treating the very poorest people of America in some slum in New Jersey. He was still hard at work in 1966 when Mama and Papa came to the States for a visit and were able to go and visit him, and he was delighted to see them.

He was smart, and lucky to have had the means to get out of Germany when he did. A lot of Jewish people left at that time as life was getting more and more difficult and dangerous for them in Nazi-occupied Germany.

There was one very cold and restless November night I remember when Mama stood by the open bedroom window listening to horrible smashing noises and loud shouting and screaming coming, not from the Altenhofer's, but from all over the city, so loud that it woke us up. This was "Krystallnacht," when Nazi hooligans were smashing, looting and burning Jewish establishments and businesses, not only in Wurzburg but all over Germany.

We went to see our Oma the next morning and there was broken glass all over the sidewalk on Sanderstrasse and Augustinerstrasse, and all the beautifully decorated show windows were now just empty, broken holes. Mama just shook her head at all this destruction and she had this really worried look on her face. She had always loved shopping at Jewish owned stores, Rutschkeweitz being her favorite. She knew when we kids desperately needed shoes and she just couldn't scrape enough money together to pay for them, this store would let her have them anyway and she would just pay a little each week until they were paid off. Very few other stores did that.

For years and years while growing up, Mama had lived next door to Jewish people, was best friends with some, babysat for them, shared in their holidays and the special foods they ate, knew all about the funny sayings they had and knew them to be kind, wonderful, very normal people. Now all of a sudden, she was supposed to think of them as the "enemy" and was supposed to shun them and even spit on them. It was insane and she just couldn't do it.

But more and more they kept their distance from us and we thought it was maybe anger, humiliation, distrust or even hatred until we learned that they were forbidden to associate with us non-Jews, as we were with them. Not all of them were rich or even well to do. They had been Germans all their lives, loving their country and just trying to eke out a living, just like the rest of us. They had no money to go somewhere else and make a fresh start and maybe they thought they could just ride out the storm. But things only got worse for them all the time.

Eventually all the borders were closed and there was no way for them to escape anymore. By then, their numbers had dwindled down quite a bit and we thought, thankfully, that they had found a way to get out of the country after all. The ones remaining were made to wear dark clothing with a big, bright yellow six-pointed star fastened to their chest, which had "Jude" (Jew) written on it. Anyone over the age of six had to wear one in public, making them targets for ridicule, insults, attacks and worse. They would just hurry along, staying close to the walls.

Mama felt so bad for them and she told us not to stare at them or even look at them, if we saw them on the street. It became increasingly rare though to see any at all. Once in a while we saw big, open trucks crammed full in the back with all these unfortunate people heading, I think, for the railroad station. Supposedly they were being deported to other countries, Palestine being the one most often mentioned. Nobody had a clue that they were actually being shipped to concentration camps where they were all gassed to death.

To this day, this is too monstrous and too revolting to comprehend! We had heard of these camps of course. Anyone who dared to speak out against the Hitler regime or opposed it in any way ended up there and was never heard from again, regardless of race, color, religion or nationality. It didn't require such "trivial" things as real evidence or proof or a trial to be put away—someone's word or suspicion was good enough. If someone had it in for you, here was a perfect way to get rid of you.

Everybody was wary of his neighbors, friends and even family members. Nobody could be fully trusted and one had to choose one's words very carefully. Children were actually encouraged to report anything they overheard at home that might be considered anti-Hitler or anti-Nazi, and some did especially if their parents wouldn't let them have their way. They were told it was for the good of the "Fatherland" to do this.

It was a dreadful thing to hear those Nazi boots approaching and the loud knock on the door when they came for somebody. They never did it quietly, because they wanted to intimidate the people with these tactics, and they did. I don't really remember it, but Mama sometimes talked about when that dreaded knock came to our door.

Papa had been treasurer for the worker's union he belonged to and he had a list of members to collect dues from every month for the union. It was not political or subversive or anything like that, just hard working men trying to get some better working conditions. When Hitler came to power, all unions were outlawed and it was forbidden to belong to one.

So one day this Nazi in full uniform, gun and all, showed up at our door demanding from Papa a list of union members. He made a big show of taking his gun out of its holster and laying it on the table for further information. But Papa steadfastly denied ever having had such a list at all and the guy finally believed him and left after what seemed like an eternity. The list meanwhile was safely tucked away in a secret drawer that was built into our living room schrank.

The union had been disbanded according to the law and Papa didn't see any need for the Nazis to know exactly who once belonged to it. No doubt it would have been used against them sooner or later—and Papa too. He was actually lucky that nothing more came of this, because it was such small acts of defiance that landed a lot of people in concentration camps.

Papa knew from the very beginning that Hitler was bad news for Germany and a lot of Germans felt that way. The first time Hitler tried to overthrow the government in 1923 he ended up in prison with a five-year sentence for treason. Because of amnesties he was released after serving much less than half that time, but it was during his imprisonment that he wrote his book, "Mein Kampf," in which he spelled out in detail all his evil plans for Germany and most of Europe.

So many people bought it that it made Hitler a millionaire, but apparently they didn't heed it or believe it. I don't know if Papa ever read the book or not, but in 1933 when Hitler ran for chancellor, Papa told Mama, "A vote for Hitler is a vote for war," so they didn't vote for him. They had been through war already with all its horror. Besides Papa, both of Mama's twin brothers had served in World War I, along with every other young, eligible man they knew. The ones that were lucky enough to come back all had their own horror stories to tell.

Nobody in their right mind would vote for war, but that is exactly what they did when they voted for Hitler. Actually there was widespread suspicion about this whole election. Rumor had it that votes that were not for Hitler were simply not counted, or declared illegal. Anyone trying to challenge it however, ended up dead or in prison. It was a tide that couldn't be stemmed. There were millions of people who supported Hitler.

He was one of the greatest orators that ever lived and his fiery speeches gave the people what they needed most at that time, which was hope for a better future. He made them feel proud to be German once again, something they hadn't felt since they lost the war in 1918. There had been no real recovery from that in all those years. First there was this terrible inflation, which robbed everybody of everything they ever owned, and then the 1929 worldwide depression struck, lasting several more years.

It was too many seemingly endless years of misery, hunger and unemployment and people were ready for a change—especially the young. I guess they would have followed the devil himself and as it turned out they did! At first, everything did get better pretty quickly. Unemployment was a thing of the past. Anyone that wanted to work found work and even those that didn't want to work had to work.

Thousands were drafted, and thousands more recruited to build the Autobahn, one of the top priorities on Hitler's agenda. This was weird since very few people had a car and therefore never would be able to use it. This was supposed to be remedied by developing and building the affordable Volkswagen for the masses. Everybody was supposed to be able to own one, but very few actually ever did as the factories were converted to building war machinery before long.

And that of course was the real purpose of the Autobahn, to be able to move troops and equipment in preparation for war. All this buildup of troops and weaponry was at first done in secret because it was in direct violation of the Versailles treaty, a treaty Germany was forced to sign when it lost the war in 1918. It prohibited Germany from any such activity as rearming at all.

Once Hitler felt strong enough and firmly in control, he declared the whole treaty illegal and null and void, and proceeded to build up a war machine such as the world had never seen before. A lot of it was financed with money and assets the Jewish people were forced to leave behind. It was all so diabolical! Of course, once he had his war machine ready, he was eager to use it and he set out to conquer Europe just as his idol Napoleon had done.

First, he made his home country Austria part of Germany and annexed the small countries on both sides of the border, such as Alsace Lorraine, Bohemia, Monrovia, Sudetenland and heaven knows what else. They were all now part of Greater Germany. When he invaded Czechoslovakia, the people there didn't like it at all, but their president was forced to sign the country over to Germany. Other countries were getting alarmed now and started warning Hitler to stay out of their territory. England sent emissaries to "appease" Hitler and warned him against further expansion, but let him keep what he had already conquered.

Of course, Hitler had much bigger plans. When he started the invasion of Poland on September 1, 1939, England and its ally France gave him an ultimatum to withdraw immediately. Hitler had no intention of doing that, so they had no choice but to declare war on Germany. And that's how it all started.

I remember young people marching through town singing and shouting "hurrah-War" like it was something to celebrate. But Mama was crying, probably one of the first times I ever saw her do that. Somehow she knew that this war would be much worse than the first one she had experienced as a young girl.

Papa, at age 39, was drafted to serve in the army, along with thousands of men even older than he, having to leave on short notice for basic training. We took the train to visit him one time just before he was shipped out to Poland. We have a picture of that visit, of all of us sitting in a beer garden in Wernfeld. This could have easily been the last time we ever saw our Papa, but thankfully it wasn't. But it was the beginning of a pretty dismal year.

We missed our Papa and our nightly ritual when he would bend over our beds and say "gut nacht, schlaf wohl, eiei-kussel" (good night, sleep well, rub cheeks together and a kiss). I still remember how his mustache tickled! No more "schankeln," no more goodies from the store and no more dancing. All the chores he had done so quietly that nobody even noticed, like bringing up coal, wood or potatoes from the basement, or cleaning out stovepipes and the ashes from the stoves or mending and pumping up bicycle tires and so many other things, Mama had to cope with now, besides everything else.

Karin and I were still pretty little, she was six, I was five, but more and more, Mama got us involved in the daily chores of life. The coal shuttle was too heavy for us, but the potatoes we had to get on a regular basis from the basement. It was pitch dark and scary down there and one of us had to carry a candle so we could see. More than once, one of us would catch our hair on fire or singe our eyebrows, or a little draft would blow out the tiny flame and we would scramble up the dark cellar steps in total panic, hanging onto each other. Eventually, we learned not to be so afraid of that basement and we carried matches so we could relight the candle.

Karola had finished her eight years of school and now worked hard, long hours as an apprentice in a small grocery store owned by a young couple, the Trabolds. Those were the days when everything was in bins, drawers and barrels behind the counter and was weighed, packaged and measured on an individual basis. Most everything was bought in small quantities then, one or two pounds or less, and put in round bags that had a point on the bottom. These had to be folded a certain way so they would stay closed and nothing would spill out. I remember Karola practicing for hours to get those folds just right and she actually got graded on them.

She went to school once a week, learning book keeping, sign making, and everything else needed to successfully manage and own a grocery store someday. She even learned calligraphy and made beautiful labels and price tags for all the merchandise, all at the ripe old age of fourteen!

This was also the year Karin had started first grade, a total bummer for me because I lost my playmate. Mama had long since quit the paper route, but she still cleaned the stores and the owners there were kind enough to allow her to bring me along, as she didn't want to leave me home alone. So after Karola went to work and Karin left for school, Mama would put me on her bike and off we would go.

The first stop was Gumbrecht, a handy crafts store that specialized in embroidery, knitting, crochet, and those kinds of things. There was a big, brightly lit room upstairs, where all these ladies sat and embroidered beautiful things for people who loved those things, but didn't have the time or talent to do it themselves. This is where they allowed me to hang out and I loved it.

One young lady especially liked me and encouraged me to draw a picture to send to her fiancée who was at the front in Russia. Imagine my surprise when he sent a letter addressed to me, thanking me for the picture, along with a color book all about soldiers and army life. Mama saved that letter for me for many years. I was so thrilled! It wasn't long after that, that this young man was killed in the war.

Another place Mama worked was Eidam next door, an electric light fixture place, the exact opposite of the first place. It was cluttered and crowded full of stuff, not only in the store, but also in the dank basement where I mostly spent my time sitting on the basement steps. Mama would come by every so often schlepping a heavy mop bucket or a broom and trash can, telling me she was almost done and then it would take another eternity before she did it again, or so it seemed.

We had to be back home by noon, because Karin would be home from school and couldn't get in. I could hardly wait to see her and find out all about school and what she had learned, making a real pest of myself. Sometimes she just wanted to be left alone and forget about school. She made friends very easily and everybody always wanted to be her friend and get together after school to play, but Mama would tell her, "you don't need friends, you have a sister," which Karin never let me forget. It wasn't fair to her and very frustrating sometimes.

Mama delivered her magazines in the afternoon on her bike. One time she took me along, but it was just too complicated. Bikes didn't have kickstands back then. So, she would have to find a place to lean it against, get me off, get her magazines out of the saddlebags, lock up the bike, haul me and the magazines upstairs to all these different doors, and wait for the money because she collected at the same time and she had to do this over and over, all over town.

It went a little bit faster without me, so she left me at home with Karin and locked us in, as she had done before. But by then both of us had an attitude and I had a very bad temper. Karin wouldn't want to play what I wanted to play and I would attack her. Or we would play board games and she would always outsmart me, making me lose, lose, lose, which made me very angry, but she would only laugh at me, which of course made me jump on her, trying to beat her up. But she was also stronger than I, just holding me at bay with her strong arms, so I would bite and scratch her. That is how I earned the nickname "Minzi," (cat).

By the time Mama came home, we would be so upset, we would meet her at the door crying and telling on each other. But Mama would not hear any of it, she just put us over her knee and gave us both a good spanking, telling us to go and console each other. Life seemed so terribly unfair back then! But we learned to get along better after a few of these times, and even if we had a spat, we wouldn't tell Mama, because it would only result in another spanking. We became co-conspirators against Mama and even developed our own way of speaking that Mama didn't understand. She didn't like it, because she thought that we were talking behind her back, which of course we were doing.

There was a certain amount of sibling rivalry going on too, of course. Karola, like so many older children, felt that we younger ones got away with a lot more than she ever did and she was probably right. Karola loved to tease Karin a lot and Karin thought it was some repressed feelings of jealousy at the same time admitting that she felt intensely jealous of me sometimes because she thought I got more attention, being the youngest. But she was always very protective of me. They both loved to tease me when I couldn't make the "sh" sound because it always came out "z."

Karin and I were jealous of the relationship between Mama and Karola, which seemed more like friends than mother and daughter. Karola never got in trouble, while we were constantly in hot water. As winter approached and the days kept getting shorter, Mama quite often would stop by at Karola's store after delivering her magazines and wait for her so Karola wouldn't have to walk home alone in the dark.

By then, the city had total blackout orders, no more streetlights, no lights from any windows, car lights and bicycle lights had to be capped so only a little slit was visible. The streetcars operated in total darkness, except for a little fluorescent paint around the edges. They used to ring a bell a lot to make people aware of their approach. Curbs and house corners and trees and lamp posts were similarly marked with a little strip of purple fluorescent paint and people took to wearing small fluorescent buttons, so they wouldn't run into each other, which they sometimes did anyway.

It was unbelievably dark out there and really weird and eerie and it took some getting used to at first. I can see why Mama didn't want Karola out there by herself. At the same time, Karin and I sat home alone in the dark just waiting for her to come home. We hadn't learned how to turn on the gas light yet and we weren't allowed to do that anyway, without first putting up the heavy canvas mats that had to be hung from hooks above the window so no light would shine through. We were too short to reach the hooks even standing on a chair.

One time Lulu came over to our door and asked if we were in there in the dark and we said yes. So he offered to turn the light on for us if we opened the door. He had figured out that the lock could be pushed back from the inside, because the whole mechanism was exposed there. Well, we let him in but then we couldn't find the mats to put on the window, so he never did light the gaslight. But we couldn't relock the door without a key.

When Mama came home she realized right away that the door was unlocked and we were in big trouble once again. Under no circumstances were we to unlock this door ever again for anybody. Karin and I were glad to know though that we had an escape route in case of an emergency. And that emergency came sooner than we ever thought possible.

We were home alone and locked in as usual. I was bouncing around on this homemade bench we had behind the kitchen table. Mama kept little pillows there for us to sit on and somehow I tripped over one and fell off the bench. My arm hit a broken jug Mama used to prop open the door sometimes, right next to that bench. It cut me in two places and I was bleeding profusely. Karin didn't know what to do, so she pushed the lock back and we ran over to see Lulu, who was also home alone with his little brothers. He was shocked to see all that blood, but tried to act very calm.

First he had me hold my arm under the running water, and then he ran and got a big slab of butter to put on my two cuts. That didn't do a whole lot of good though. Apparently I hadn't cut any major arteries and eventually it stopped bleeding. Our mothers came home together soon after that and Mama wasn't even mad that we had pushed the lock back and Lulu didn't get in trouble for wasting the butter. It was odd.

But here I was with two big gashes in my skinny little arm, and something had to be done. Reluctantly Mama took me to see Dr. Mertz, who lived just up the street on Sonderstrasse and was the only doctor in the area since Dr. Strauss left. This was the doctor who "killed Rita," my cousin. Not intentionally of course, but with incompetence, and he proved his total incompetence once again by simply covering my gashes with a couple of band aids, no stitches—not even butterflies to pull the gashes together, leaving me with two big scars on my arm for the rest of my life. Mama could have done that.

But there was another reason Mama was reluctant to see him, which I only learned many years later. Not long after Papa had to go to Poland, I had my first episode of nosebleeds. My nose started bleeding and they couldn't get it to stop for many hours. I was just a skinny little thing then and didn't have that much blood to spare. Mama was really worried and she sent someone to go get Dr. Mertz. He came, but had no real solution of what to do but she had the distinct feeling that he was coming onto her (what a sleazebag!).

I was totally unaware of what was going on, but I know I had a very restless night and every time I woke up I saw Mama and Oma sitting by my bed praying and there was a candle burning, which was the only light in the room. I thought I was probably going to die, but I made it through the night somehow. The next morning a taxi came to take Mama and me to the Luitpold Krankenhaus, the university hospital on the other side of town. We had no way to call a taxi so I suspect the doctor must have sent it. It was actually the first time I ever rode in a car and it should have been a real thrill, but I was so weak, I hardly noticed.

Some doctors examined me and talked about packing my nose full of cotton and I wondered how in the world would I breathe? But my nose had finally stopped bleeding, so they didn't do anything. It was a total waste of time and money for the taxi. We took the streetcar home, which meant we had to walk some distance up a hill first, but Mama didn't have enough money for another taxi.

With Papa gone, Mama drew even closer to her family. We stopped by at our Oma's and Opa's pretty often now and Oma was always delighted to see us, telling Opa, "Look our girls are here," with a big smile on her face. They had a big, dark kitchen with a slanted wall like ours, and Opa would be sitting by the one and only little window in an old wicker chair, smoking a pipe and trying to read the newspaper.

Oma had a standard little joke, she would tell Karin in a very loud whisper to go get the scissors and cut off Opa's bushy moustache. Karin took it seriously and found the scissors and climbed up in his lap, with Opa laughing and fending her off, until Mama took the scissors away. She told her Oma was only joking and not to get the scissors anymore, so we would just climb on his lap and pull his moustache, with him laughing the whole time.

Oma thought he needed a little cheering up. Ever since they moved to Wurzburg, practically all his life he had always worked for Jewish people, sort of as an all around handyman, doing whatever needed doing. Now that they were all gone, he was at loose ends and didn't know what to do. He was over seventy years old by then and he never actually worked again.

And they had another big heartache.

Otto, their mentally handicapped son, who was in his thirties by then, started having episodes of being hard to control and even got very violent at times. Oma and Opa thought they could handle him, but it got more difficult each time. Finally a neighbor reported it and Otto was taken away and placed in a mental institute in Werneck. This was close enough that Oma could catch the train in the morning, spend some time with him, and come home in the evening and he seemed happy and content there (although he was probably medicated).

Everybody thought that this was the best solution for all concerned and it worked quite well for a good while. But of course, Hitler had no use for "those kind of people." Oma was preparing for another visit with Otto, when she got a notice that he had been transferred to a hospital far away, near the eastern border because Werneck was being shut down.

This was terrible news for Oma. Even though she had Hanni after Otto, he was and would always be her baby, due to his mental state. Now she couldn't even communicate with him because he couldn't read or write. She would send cards and little packages with goodies, but had no way of knowing if he even got them. When she couldn't stand it anymore, she made the long, arduous trip by train to see him. When she got to the city she had to find her way around to the hospital and find a place to stay overnight.

It was hard for an old woman by herself and cost money she couldn't afford, but she needed to see him and make sure he was okay. The little form letters she got from the hospital every now and then, saying he was doing fine just weren't very convincing to her. Physically he was fine, but he was terribly homesick and wanted desperately to go home with her. It really broke her heart to have to leave him there, knowing it would be a long time before she could make the trip again. She never did.

Shortly after she got back, not even a week later, they were notified that Otto had died of pneumonia and had been cremated. It was inconceivable—another innocent victim of the Nazis! The hospital was shut down shortly thereafter because all the mental patients had "died of pneumonia," and they all were cremated before anyone could see them, and all this without their family's consent. After a while, Oma and Opa received an urn, which supposedly contained Otto's ashes and we had a nice funeral for him with all his siblings and extended family and friends present. (I remember this funeral.) And now we had another grave to visit, which we did quite often, always bringing flowers.

Six

Try as I might, I cannot remember that first Christmas without Papa. It had to be very hard for Mama, for he was the one who put up the tree and the manger and helped to make it all so festive for us. Somehow, she must have managed to do it all by herself and with Karola's help, make it really nice ore else I surely would remember it.

I definitely remember Easter because it was such a disaster. We had been invited to spend it with Uncle Sepp and Tante Kattel in Schweinfurt. Uncle Sepp was Papa's only living relative then and Mama did her best to make him feel welcome whenever he came to Wurzburg on business, which he did pretty often. She would fix a nice meal, after which he would smoke a big, fat cigar, befitting the image of the big shot businessman he thought he was.

His business was at first a small hardware and house wares store his wife's father had owned. This was right up Uncle Sepp's alley since the trade he had learned as a young boy was metal and iron works. Together, they developed this little shop into a successful and profitable bicycle shop building racing and specialty bikes for some of Germany's most famous bikers.

Tante Kattel, his wife, was somewhat of a character, very funny and down to earth. She had bright red hair and her face was completely covered in freckles. She walked with a strange gait and slurred her words sometimes, which became more pronounced with age. Everyone thought she might be having a drinking problem, but no one ever saw her doing that and she didn't seem to drink.

It all became clear several years later when she was diagnosed with multiple sclerosis. She had been in the beginning stages of this disease way back then and it steadily progressed and she became completely disabled and after many, many years of suffering it finally proved fatal. To Uncle Sepp's credit, I have to say that he took care of her at home all those years with no outside help at all. But of course all this came much later. Back then, she was just our funny, quirky aunt, who had invited us for Easter.

We caught the train Saturday afternoon, loaded down with all sorts of good things to eat. Mama never went anywhere empty-handed, especially now since food was strictly rationed. She didn't want to be a burden to anybody. She had baked a cake to take and had gotten ham and I don't know what all, leaving our cupboard and her wallet pretty bare.

All went well until Sunday morning when Uncle Sepp got ready for church and wanted to know who else was going. The women wanted to stay home and cook dinner, but we girls had to go because Mama thought it wouldn't look right if we didn't. Mama was always extremely concerned about how we appeared to other people.

Actually, we were terribly shy and self-conscious, especially around people we didn't see too often. If we did warm up a little and she thought we were getting out of line, she was quick to discipline and slap us, embarrassing us and making us even shyer around people. We don't use the expression, "children should be seen but not heard," in Germany but it was definitely practiced back then.

Anyway, we went to church and it was cold and crowded and we had to stand the whole time. Uncle Sepp seemed to know everybody there and greeted a lot of people, among them a woman with extremely bowed legs. As she walked past us, Karin apparently turned to see if they were just as bowed in back (they were). She didn't know that she shouldn't have done that. I don't even know if Uncle Sepp said anything to her, but when we got back to the house, he jumped all over Mama about how badly we had embarrassed him. As a businessman in the community, he couldn't afford to be embarrassed that way, and on and on he went.

Mama was at first mortified and then she realized he was totally over-reacting and told him so. They both said some harsh things and next thing you know, we were on the train back to Wurzburg, leaving all our good food behind. We didn't even get dinner. All the stores were closed on Sunday and Monday too because of the holiday. So, even if we had money and food stamps, we couldn't buy anything.

I don't really remember, but I guess we ate potatoes again for least we had plenty of them. This was our one and only overnight visit with Uncle Sepp and Tante Kattel and their son Rudy, who was somewhat older than Karola and therefore didn't have much in common with us young kids and mostly ignored us.

After that experience we stayed closer to home, Mama's brothers Karl and Fritz being older than Papa had escaped this round of drafting for now, so we used to visit them frequently. Though they were twins, they were very different in appearance and temperament. Karl was tall and slim with black hair and blue eyes, very friendly and laid back, and a shoemaker by trade. He owned his own shoe repair shop for a while, but it didn't bring in enough money to support his family adequately, so he ended up working for the brewery where Oma worked.

He was married to Marie, a native of southern Bavaria, where they speak with the cutest accent. We loved listening to her talk, which she did a lot. She was very outgoing and always very happy to see us. Like Mama and Papa, they had an older daughter, Mahlehen, a couple of years older than Karola, and then about seven or eight years later, they had Friedel, about two years older than Karin. Mahlehen had the black hair and blue eyes like her dad, our Uncle Karl. She was a very pretty girl and just as friendly, but we didn't get to see her very often. Like Karola, she was working at a young age and at age seventeen, like all German girls at that age, she was drafted into the "arbeitsdienst," the military service for women.

No one really had a clue where Uncle Karl's and Mahlehen's exotic good looks originated. Rumor had it that our Oma in her younger years had been a beautiful woman with black hair, but she had dark brown eyes to match. No pictures of her in her youth exist, though. As long as I knew her, she was a somewhat gaunt, toothless old woman with her gray hair tightly coiled in a little bun on top of her head, and always wearing very dark colored dresses. She steadfastly resisted having dentures made, because she said she didn't need them, she could eat anything she wanted, even apples, just by gumming them. Actually she looked exactly like a grandma was supposed to look back then. Everybody else's grandma looked and dressed like that, and we loved her very much.

Karl was really the only "odd" one of her children, all the rest of the clan looked like Kemmers, Opa's side of the family, with brown hair and grayish eyes, kind of stocky in build and quite average in looks. Friedel was definitely a Kemmer, but she was always very nice to us and played with us, while Mama and her parents were visiting. We were guests at her First Communion and there are pictures of that in the photo album. We still exchange Christmas cards.

They lived in a small apartment in the Frankfurterstrasse, across the Main River and we usually took the streetcar to go see them, because it was a pretty good distance. Uncle Fritz lived even further away, also across the river, but in a different direction. Unfortunately, no streetcar went that way, so we just had to hike to go see him. Like Mama, he definitely was a Kemmer in looks and kind of gruff in mannerism, a man of few words.

He and his wife Tante Gretel lived in a small house in the middle of a big garden, almost like a mini-farm. They grew most everything they ate and ate most everything they grew, but sometimes they had too much of things like gooseberries and red currants and other fruits and vegetables that we gladly and gratefully took off their hands. They also had chickens and geese and a pig they were fattening for slaughter, and they had a goat that gave more milk than they knew what to do with. Mama gladly took that too for us.

One whole summer, Karola rode her bike out there every evening to go get the milk, which Mama turned into hot cocoa or oatmeal or whatever. She made the berries into marmalade to put on bread and they were delicious straight from the bush. Sometimes they even let us help pick them.

There were a lot of reasons why we loved to visit Uncle Fritz and Tante Gretel, and one big one was the swing Uncle Fritz had built. It was just an ordinary wood frame with a board suspended by thick ropes or chains—I don't remember which. I just remember what a heavenly feeling it was to swing on this swing. Of course we always asked for permission first and then we had to take turns because Karin loved it as much as I did.

Uncle Fritz hadn't built it for us. When Fritz and Gretel got married, she was a widow with two children, Adam and Eva, who were grown, by the time I came along. Eva had a daughter named Anneliese, who was a year or two younger than me. She was Fritz and Gretel's granddaughter, and it was for her that Uncle Fritz built the swing. They doted on that little girl.

In our opinion she was a totally spoiled, selfish little brat. Every time we got on that swing, by the time we got the hang of it, she made us get off, because she wanted to swing, but then she quickly got bored with it. Being an only child, she just didn't understand the concept of sharing or taking turns, like Karin and I. We actually couldn't enjoy something unless the other one was enjoying it too and we shared everything.

But we played with Anneliese and she loved the attention we showered on her, and in between, we also got in a little "swinging time" on her swing. She got so attached to us that one time she wanted to go home with us when it was time for us to leave. Mama had misgivings right from the start, but Anneliese begged and pleaded, until everybody agreed to let her come home with us and spend the night. Mama even let us sleep in her and Papa's big bed, so the three of us could be together.

All was well until one o'clock in the morning, when Anneliese woke up and wanted her grandma, crying hysterically. She actually got up and ran for the door, which of course was locked, thank goodness. Nothing we said or tried had any effect at all, she wanted her grandma and she cried most of the night until she finally fell back asleep. There was no way we could take her home in the middle of the night, but Mama promised to do it first thing in the morning and she kept her word, even though by then Anneliese had changed her mind and didn't want to go home.

Mama had no time or patience for fickle behavior like that, especially after keeping everybody up all night. She felt like this kid needed a good spanking, but thankfully she restrained herself. Needless to say, this was our only sleepover with Anneliese or anyone else for that matter. People lived in such close, cramped quarters back then, that sleepovers such as children enjoy today, were unheard of and impossible and just weren't done. We all went home and slept in our own bed at night no matter how late it got or how far it was.

The people we went to visit more than anyone else in those days were Mama's sister Marie and her "gang," our cousins Betty, Karola, and Rudi. Her husband, our Uncle Willie, who was the same age as Papa, was also drafted as was their older son Karl. With all the men gone to war, the women clung to each other more than ever. Every Sunday, right after dinner, which was served promptly at noon, as soon as the dishes were washed, we headed out to go see Tante Marie. This meant a good one-hour walk, a lot of it uphill.

Tante Marie, after many years of living in dumpy little places in town, had rented a place in a small house just barely inside the city limits up on the hill next to the Flugplatz, the Wurzburg airfield. The hill was named "Galgenberg," or Gallows Hill, as years and years earlier that's where criminals were put to death by hanging. It was a cold, barren wind swept place.

When it became an airfield, a huge area was fenced in and later, when the German air force took it over, the fence was extended even further, all the way to Tante's house. It had barbed wire placed on top and airmen patrolled the perimeter with guard dogs. No one seemed to know what these airmen were guarding. Way across a wide open field inside the fence one could see some planes sometimes and there was a runway and hangars and other buildings with camouflage paint on the roofs. There also were some round pillboxes serving as anti-aircraft or "flak" stations, scattered all throughout the fields outside the fence.

The road to Tante's house ran all along this fence with only a shallow ditch separating the two. The other side of this two-lane paved country road was also flanked by a shallow ditch and beyond that were vast fields of wheat and potatoes, no buildings, no trees, not even shrubs, just wide, open spaces. Some of it was so steep that it was impossible to pedal a bike up, one had to get off and push. But closer to the house the road evened out for a good little stretch and started going downhill just past the house, gradually at first, until it reached a very steep hill going down into the village of Gerbrunn.

The little house that Tante rented was actually a companion to a much bigger two-story house, which at one time had been a guesthouse, the "Gasthaus zum kirschbaum" (cherry tree guest house). The two houses were separated by a beer garden, which was shaded by walnut trees and horse chestnut trees, not cherry trees—but there were lots of cherry, apple, plum and pear trees in the area surrounding the little village. In the front, the beer garden was shielded from the road by a long row of lilac bushes, which extended al the way to the front of the little house. It was quite idyllic, like an oasis—after that long, barren road.

That of course had been its original purpose, a hiker's destination. Germany had lots of those kinds of places. People loved to hike somewhere on Sundays or holidays, have some refreshments and then hike back. One definitely needed refreshments after walking that long, dusty road with no shade, no shelter, with the sun beating down, the wind howling across the wide, open fields, and nothing particularly interesting to look at. No one in their right mind would walk there, unless they had to and that's why the guesthouse ultimately failed. There were lots of much prettier and more hospitable places to walk to in Wurzburg. In a better location, it might have been a big success.

It may have been intended to be a true guesthouse or hotel at first, since all the rooms upstairs had separate doors to the landing. The little house next door was built to be a dance hall but when that failed, it was converted into two-room apartments with a long hallway separating them, with no basement, no attic, no insulation, and no indoor plumbing. The only source of water was a spigot at the end of the hallway with a bucket underneath. All used water was simply flung across the fence to the Flugplatz, which ran about six feet from the front door. There was an honest to goodness outhouse, a wooden box with flies and all, behind the house.

When Tante Marie moved there, at least one other family lived there already, possibly even two, but eventually they all moved out and Tante took over the whole house. It was infinitely better than any other place she ever lived in, never mind the inconvenience of being so far from everything and the terribly cold winters she had to endure in that house when she could only afford to heat one room, and it never really got warm. There would be ice crystals on the walls, even with the stove doing all it could do.

Onkel Willi had at long last finally gotten his act together and was working regularly, resulting in a much better financial situation for them. He even owned a motorcycle with a sidecar, the next best thing to owning a car, making the trip into town a breeze. The problem was, when he was drafted, no one else was licensed or knew how to drive that heavy machine and it sat idle for the duration.

No one would ever accuse Tante Marie of working too hard. She never actually had a paying job, rather she would spend her day reading romance novels and embroidering tablecloths and pillowcases, things Mama never had time to do. Once a week, on Saturday, she would come to town with Rudi to shop for fresh supplies, stopping by at our place to eat and rest before making the long trek back. She would bring a big package of a wonderful variety of lunchmeats and crispy fresh rolls and pickles and she would even offer us some, but we were usually too shy to accept, even though we were secretly drooling.

Betty and Karola, who were both working in town, would come by after work to help Tante haul home all the things she had bought. I can't say for sure, but I believe they had bicycles, which of course made the trip to town a lot easier. It was tremendous fun and downright thrilling to come down all those smaller hills and especially that last big one. Mama liked taking the bikes to see Tante Marie, even if we did have to mostly push them there, for the simple reason that it was quicker to come home in the evening. By then, Karola had outgrown her little bike and had gotten a full-size one and Karin used the little bike.

I was still riding in the baby seat on Mama's bike but I was getting pretty heavy for Mama to pedal both of us and my legs were getting too long and getting in the way. One time, Karin and Rudi were determined to teach me how to ride that little bike, and the road in front of Tante's house was ideal for that, nice and smooth and straight, with no traffic. They would both run beside me holding onto my seat and handlebars until I got steady enough that Rudi could only hold onto my seat (or so I thought). Then I got so cocky that I turned loose one hand to wave at Karin and ended up in the ditch. Rudi hadn't been holding me at all, I had been riding it all by myself and it was fun. But we only had the one small bike, so we had to take turns with it.

Going home, it was tricky and took a certain amount of know-how to come down that really steep hill, because halfway down, one had to make a right angle turn to the left and go down another steep hill. One time Karin took the turn a little bit too fast and her wheels spun right out from under her, wiping her out big time. Mama had a hard time stopping her bike to go back and help Karin with my added weight on it. Poor Karin's knees and hands and elbows were all scraped up and bloody and she was limping along pushing her bike, Mama and me beside her. But eventually she got back on and rode the rest of the way home. She was such a brave girl!

Soon after that, we stopped taking the bikes and just walked. In spite of the distance we really loved our Sunday afternoons at Tante Marie's. Mama often brought a cake, but Tante usually had some kind of delicious cake for us also. Living so close to the village where fruit grew in abundance, it was usually flat sheet cake with fruit on top—rhubarb being the earliest of the season, then cherries and peaches and later plums and apples and berries or buttery crumbs with cinnamon if no fruit was available.

It is amazing how well everything turned out, considering she only had a wood and coal-burning stove with no thermostat or any way to control the heat. It was all strictly guesswork and apparently Tante had it down quite well. Sometimes she set up her kitchen table out on the lawn between the little house and the lilac bushes, under a tree that Rudi liked to climb. She would serve steaming hot coffee out of her big porcelain coffee pot to drink with the cake, ours would have lots of milk and sugar in it, or she would have lemonade for us kids.

It was obvious that all the ladies, Mama, Tante Marie, Betty and the two Karolas, enjoyed each other's company immensely and they would linger over their "kaffee klatsch" all afternoon, while we kids—Karin, Rudi and I, newly refreshed—were eager to go roaming and exploring. Behind the little house next to the outhouse, Tante had a bunch of rabbit hutches for all the rabbits she was breeding, not for pets but for food and also for their fur. It was Rudi's job to help feed them and clean out the hutches. He would let us hold some of the babies sometimes and they were so cute, but he told us right away not to get attached as they would surely end up on our dinner table some day, and they did. Every Christmas, Mama made "hasenpfeffer," out of one of Tante's rabbits for our big Christmas dinner, which was Tante's gift to our family.

Rudi was a pretty unique individual. Even at this young age, he displayed a self-confidence and independence that Karin and I could only marvel at. We didn't know it then, but his sisters thought he was a holy terror who needed a much stronger hand than his mother provided. The word "no" was not in Tante's vocabulary, where Rudi was concerned and he pretty well did as he pleased even then. But he was fun and exciting to us, because we never knew what he was going to come up with next. It was he who led us to the anti-aircraft stations, which were unmanned at the time, to take a closer look.

And it was also he who showed us one at the time graphic pictures of where babies really come from. Heaven only knows where he got those pictures. Mama had no clue and we certainly didn't tell her that we already knew when several years later she finally had that "talk" with us. Those were things we didn't like to talk about, not with Rudi, not with Mama, not even with each other. We were just too shy and embarrassed.

All the while, I was eagerly looking forward to starting first grade in spite of Rudi's dire warning that school was a whole other ballgame. What he actually said was, "Da gehts aus einem andern Fassle," which translated doesn't make any sense. It was no secret that Rudi didn't like school very much. He attended Schillerschule, a good hour's walk away and I'm sure that the distance had a lot to do with his dislike of school. Being two years older, he seemed big to me, but he really wasn't then. I can't even imagine a little boy walking along that long lonely road every day, all by himself in every kind of weather. No other kids lived near him so he was strictly on his own.

But he seemed to be taking it all in stride. Sometimes he got side tracked along the way, as little boys tend to do, chasing frogs or lizards or cute little hedgehogs that roll up into a prickly ball when they feel threatened. So he would arrive late at school. Rather than go in and face the music, he would just simply skip school all together. Instead, he would hang out at the park, watching the ducks and the goldfish and feeding them part of his sandwich his mom always packed for him. Wurzburg's many, many church bells ringing in the noontime hour told him when it was time to head home.

Since no one had a phone back then, the school had no way of checking up on truant children, but they diligently kept track of all the absences and marked them on his report card and that's how Tante Marie found out about it. Missing so much school of course made it hard for him to keep up and his grades reflected that, but somehow he squeaked by and never flunked a grade. Overall, he was one of the kindest, most laid-back persons I have ever known, remaining cool, calm and collected in every situation and even though his mother worried about him a lot, he was also a great comfort to her and he turned out just fine in the end.

The school year started in spring back then, after a lengthy Easter vacation, usually sometime in April or very early May, so my turn came soon after I had turned six years old in March 1940. School was tough from the very first day, so to "sweeten" that first day, some children got "Zuckertute" from their parents, literally translated it was a "sugar bag," actually a tall, brightly decorated cardboard cone filled with all sorts of sweets—almost as tall as the little first graders themselves.

We saw them displayed in the store windows along with schools supplies, and proudly shown off by those who got one and brought it to school the first day. This is one custom that still survives to this day in Germany, probably even more so now than back then, when fewer people could afford such things. Karola hadn't gotten a Zuckertute and neither did Karin, so I knew I wasn't going to get one either and I was right, but Mama made sure I had a nice, new dress to wear and a new pair of shoes. A lot of kids didn't even have that.

Nearly half my classmates came from the "Kaserne," a massive four-story tall building that had at one time been an army barracks. It actually had quite an interesting history and was designed by a famous builder, Balthazar Heumann. He had built the Residenz and many other beautiful buildings and churches not only in Wurzburg, but all over Bavaria. The Kaserne was built as part of the wall that surrounded Wurzburg at one time and shielded it effectively against intruders coming from the Main River, at the same time serving as a wall against flooding. The side facing the river had no windows or only very tiny ones high up, and except for one small passage way at one end, there were no doors on that side.

My street, Landwehrstrasse and its parallels Korngasse, Rosengasse and Reibletsgasse, all ended at the Kaserne and one had to walk the length of this fortress to the end where there once was a heavy wooden gate, to get to the river. When it wasn't needed for the troops anymore, it was turned into housing for very low-income people, probably the closest thing to slums Wurzburg ever had. They were dank, dismal two-room affairs with everybody sharing one spigot in the hall and a couple of toilets on the second floor. All the windows on the bottom floor had iron bars, like a prison, which is probably where some of the inhabitants came from or belonged.

But we knew some nice people there too, like the sad young widow, Frau Bonfig, whose husband had died suddenly and left her with no income and several little girls to raise, or the Sauer family, Schorsch and Betty, and their daughter Mushi and son Bubi. Schorsch was a colleague of Papa's from the old shoe repair shop, a happy-go-lucky, carefree fellow, and a real charmer with the ladies, with a big thirst for beer, wine and schnaps. He never aspired to be anything more than a shoe repairman. It was his hard working wife Betty who Mama became lifelong friends with and they were still in touch with each other when they both were over eighty years old.

There was a certain stigma attached to living in the Kaserne. Muschi, their daughter escaped it by getting married at a young age to a well-off man more than twice her age. Bubi, who was two years older than I, had the added stigma of having milk white skin and fire red hair, a pretty unusual sight in this tough neighborhood and kids would taunt him mercilessly. Having no friends at all, he threw himself with gusto into learning to play the accordion his mother had bought him and he became really good at it and I guess it was a form of escape for him.

He was so painfully shy that Karin and I had trouble getting him to talk to us whenever he visited with his mom. But we would get him to join in our board or card games and gradually he would warm up a little and we discovered that he had a fine sense of humor and could be quite funny. Of course, next time he came over we would have to start all over again trying to coax him out of his shell.

One large family in the Kaserne who provided the area with endless gossip and amusement, was the Dehlers. It wasn't because they had a lot of kids, lots of people at the Kaserne had lots of children, but because Herr Dehler, the father of all those Dehler children was nearly eighty years old at that time. In our innocence, Karin and I didn't really understand how remarkable it was for a man of that age to still be fathering babies every year. What made it more interesting to us was the fact that Herr Dehler was also Frau Altenhofer's father who had deserted his large family and divorced his first wife years earlier and was now married to a woman younger than his daughter.

Divorce was such an unusual thing back then, that people only whispered about it like it was shameful and embarrassing, and the Dehlers were the only people in the whole world as far as we knew that had ever been through one. Frau Altenhofer was not on speaking terms with her father or his young wife and it would irk her to no end to see this woman year after year strutting up Landwehrstrasse very visibly pregnant or pushing a baby carriage with a brand new baby in it.

But she would laugh it off and make fun of the situation, saying that all these poor babies looked old, gray and wrinkled just like their dad.

One of the older girls, a classmate of Karin's, had made it a habit for a while to hang around and watch when we were playing outside. She would have the new baby in the carriage and some of the other little ones in tow, so she wasn't able to participate in our games. But this gave Frau Altenhofer ample opportunity to sneak a peak at these half siblings of hers. It is anybody's guess if the girl was aware of the connection or what was going on. I almost hate to say it, but she really wasn't very bright, as was the case with a lot of the kids from the Kaserne. Somehow, extreme poverty just seems to go hand-in-hand with dullness of mind and spirit in so many cases.

Of course, we were very far from being rich ourselves, but we had parents who loved to read and who instilled that same love in us kids. And they made sure that we had good reading material. There were no free public libraries in Germany back then and inexpensive paperbacks didn't exist, so every book we owned was an investment and something to treasure.

We didn't have big birthday parties either back then, but Mama always made our day special by baking a cake the night before and setting a special place for us in the morning with one of her beautiful Rosenthal china cups for us to drink out of, and she always had some fresh flowers on the table and nobody would be allowed to yell at or be mean to the birthday child all day long.

Our only present quite often would be our very own new book that we got to read before anybody else in the family, and that was the best present of all. Coming from a family of readers, and also learning along with Karin, I guess I really had a good head start and I remember reading things in the newspaper when I was still in first grade—and I don't mean comics. German papers didn't have a comic section.

In reading class it was downright painful to listen to some of those kids from the Kaserne struggling with every syllable and word. Chances are that they never held a book in their hand and nobody ever read to them in their whole life. It was very tempting, but not a good idea to go on and read ahead because if the teacher suddenly called on someone else and they didn't pick up at the right place, they were in big trouble and would be punished. School was strictly about learning and discipline, fun and playing were not allowed at all. Most of the teachers were old, retired spinsters who had been called back from retirement because all the younger ones were now involved in some capacity or another in the war effort.

We were all zoned into Peterschule, which was a good block past Sonderstrasse, about a ten to fifteen minute walk from home. The four-story building was L-shaped with a big entrance gate close to the corner. The left wing was for the girls, and the right wing for the boys and everything was strictly segregated by gender. Boys even had a different recess time than girls. We would hear them down below, since our classrooms were on the second floor, but we would never see them.

I think it was mainly because the schoolyard was too small for all the children at one time. It was just a paved square formed by the "L" of the building with tall, stone walls on the other two sides. There was no grass or playground equipment of any kind and unless the sun was directly overhead, it didn't even shine down in there. But, unless it was pouring rain, we had to go down there and walk around while eating our sandwich, no running was allowed. Actually we had to line up two by two and march together quietly down the stairs and back up the stairs. We also had to go to the bathroom that way if we needed to or not.

Only on special days like Hitler's birthday, April 20th, or other memorable Nazi Party days, the whole school, boys and girls, would assemble in the schoolyard all neatly lined up by classes to listen to people making long and very boring speeches. Then everybody would sing "Die Fahne Hoch," (The Flag Raised High), which was one of the first songs we learned in school, along with the German anthem, "Deutschland Uber Alles."

We were too little to really understand the meaning of the words, but we memorized them anyway and the songs had a catchy tune, so we sang them with great enthusiasm. The flag song was actually the Nazi's main song, describing and glorifying how Hitler came to power and to this day it is outlawed in Germany. The schoolyard would be wall to wall with kids, and it was woefully inadequate to do anything but stand there, and that's why I think we didn't all have recess at the same time.

Apparently there was a shortage of classrooms and teachers also, so they crammed more kids into each room. We sat on long benches that had a writing surface or desk in front, four to a bench and there were two rows at least five or six deep, having room for at least forty kids! The teacher's desk was up front on a podium, two or three steps higher than the rest of the room, giving her a good oversight of the whole room.

Children were raised to be very obedient and to respect and even fear adults back then, so there wasn't much of a behavioral problem, but even minor infractions were severely punished. Absurd as it may sound, it wasn't allowed to be left handed; everyone had to use his right hand for writing and everything else. Karin, being left-handed had a hard time with that. At home she used her left hand for everything because it felt more natural to her, but at school she had to use her right hand.

Every teacher owned a thin rod that was used not only to point to things on the blackboard or the big map hanging on the wall, but also to be slammed down on a desk, sometimes just inches away from whomever's attention may have wandered a little bit. Really bad girls were called or dragged to the front of the room where they had to hold out their hands palms up to be hit with the rod three or six times, depending on the seriousness of the infraction or the teacher's mood. The rod would be whistling through the air, a truly terrifying sound and obviously it was excruciatingly painful, but crying was considered shameful and not allowed. A child that couldn't stop crying was made to stand outside the door until she stopped, which better not be very long or she would be punished some more.

For the most part, this harsh treatment seemed to work because everyone was deathly afraid of the teacher and tried to do right and be as good as they could possibly be, including me of course. But there were other ways of inflicting pain and shame. My first grade teacher was seventy-two year old Frl. Ewald (Frl. is short for "Fraulein," which means she never married), a tiny white-haired woman who never smiled and who had absolutely no love or patience for little six year olds, especially me—or so it seemed to me.

She didn't like the way I spoke, which was very slow back then and I had that little lisp that wouldn't let me make the "sh" sound. So, whenever she called on me to say something in class, she would ridicule me and ape the way I spoke. This of course made the whole class laugh at me, making me want to crawl into the nearest mouse hole. There were other girls in my class who spoke very slowly, especially one of them, Helga Keitel, who even still talked baby talk, but Frl. Ewald didn't ridicule her.

I just couldn't understand why she singled me out this way and I would go home crying to Mama about it. Mama said the teacher didn't do it to Helga because her Papa was a Hauptman (captain) in the German army, which was true. He would walk Helga all the way to her seat every morning, dressed in his fancy uniform, shiny boots, medals and all. My Papa was just a lowly railroad worker, so Mama said I was fair game. I can't say that this made me feel any better. I had never thought of my beloved Papa as being "lowly" or that it mattered at all what one's father did for a living.

There was no getting away from Frl. Ewald as she taught every subject except religion. The priest came in for that once or twice a week. My only hope was to get someone nicer in second grade, but unfortunately that didn't happen. Fr. Ewald moved on up to second grade along with us, and the same thing happened again when it was time for us to move up to third grade. The whole time she never lightened up or got any friendlier. If anything, she got tougher and stricter.

It had to be a tough job for such an old woman to cram all those basics into so many dense little heads and keep order and control at the same time. Besides the three "R's" reading, writing, and arithmetic, she taught us where in the world we were by means of geography and she taught us very recent German history—all about Hitler and his "heroes." We even learned basic knitting from Frl. Ewald in our handicraft class. And she also taught singing.

It was a full schedule considering we only went from 8:00am to 12:00pm, with one fifteen-minute break in between. There really was no time to play or even color pictures.Crayons are an American invention so we never had any. We had colored pencils but they weren't used in school until we got older. Then we used them to color in maps that we had to draw.

I can't really remember when we first started using pencils. Our basic equipment the first few years were slates with lines on one side for writing and squares on the other side for numbers. Everybody had a wooden box with a sliding lid, full of thin chalk pencils for writing on the slate. Mama sharpened ours with a small pocketknife to a fine point for neater writing. The frame of the slate had a hole, so one could tie a string to it, the other end of which had a sponge or rag tied to it for wiping the slate. It was typical German efficiency—no wasted paper.

We started out learning to write the old German way, which was quite different from how we write today. This practice was discontinued a few years after I started school—a great loss in a way. Soon there won't be any one left who can read the original manuscripts of such great writers as Schiller and Goethe, or even the writings of their own ancestors. It is a definite plus to have learned and still be able to read the old writing.

We learned the modern way of writing in the third grade, but we called it the "Latin way" for some reason. Some time before that, probably in second grade, we were introduced to "schonschreiben" (beautiful writing) with pen and ink in a notebook. The big emphasis in this class was neatness, which was trickier than it sounds. Ballpoint pens didn't exist yet and fountain pens were new and very expensive and therefore not used by children.

We used long slender wooden holders with a groove in the front into which we inserted a metal tip, which we called a Feder (feather). I guess it referred to the days when people really did write with feathers, or quills, not all that long ago. This was dipped into little bottles of ink, a disaster waiting to happen. If one forgot to scrape most of the ink back off after dipping, instead of beautiful writing, one would end up with big, ugly ink blobs in the notebook—not a good thing.

It was actually in this class that I first became aware of my better than average ability to remember things. Frl. Ewald would read a sentence to us, which we were required to write as neatly as possible into our notebook with pen and ink, no problem for me. But while concentrating on dipping and scraping their pens and writing beautifully, a lot of kids would forget what they were supposed to write after the first or second word. They would turn to me because I always remembered every word the teacher had said. Somehow it would just echo in my mind. This gift, for which I am so very thankful, has served me well through the years and is helping me right now and it even helped me win some friends back then.

When we weren't writing or holding a book or knitting needles, we had to sit with our arms folded across our chest to keep from fidgeting. And when an adult entered the room we had to stand up and say "Heil Hitler" in unison. We made a little sing song out of it, starting low with "Heil," raising our voices for "Hit" and trailing off with "ler." Proper etiquette required that we remained standing until an adult gave us permission to sit down.

One of the more humiliating things Frl. Ewald did to us was when she checked us for lice. I can still see her holding a chalk pencil or Federholder

71

with two fingers at the very end, using the other end far away from her hand to flip up our hair to check around our ears and neck. Thank goodness I never had any! Those few that did, usually kids from the Kaserne, got a note to take home and they weren't allowed to come back until they were properly deloused.

What was worse though was when the health department came to school once a year. Class by class, we would be herded into this big, nearly empty room upstairs where a bunch of people in white coats were waiting for us. Quickly, we had to take all our clothes off, pile them on a long bench or table by the wall and then parade in front of the white coats one by one alphabetically.

We were weighed and measured and looked over on all sides. I guess they were looking for malnutrition and other problems. They also tested our hearing and eyesight, and why we couldn't at least keep our panties on is beyond me. Everybody would be standing around cold and embarrassed, trying not to look at each other, while our teeth were chattering. There was very little interaction between the teachers and the parents, so I don't really know how Mama knew when they had the inspections, but she knew and she always made sure that we wore decent underwear.

We wore long cotton stockings back then that were held up by garters or long elastic strips that were attached to a bodice—something like a training bra without cups. Under this, we wore undershirts made of cotton. Our underpants were thick fleece that stretched from our waist down to below where the stockings ended, keeping our body warm underneath our dress in the cold winters of Germany. It was a lot of stuff to take off and put back on and the whole time it was "hurry, hurry, hurry," to make room for the next group. Since my last name started with "S" back then, I was always one of the last ones to get done. The whole class would be lined up ready to go back to the classroom and Frl. Ewald would be impatiently pacing back and forth, eyeing us few who weren't done yet, disapprovingly.

I remember one time Mama had me wear a brand new sky blue pair of fleece bloomers, which of course I had to take off and leave with the rest of my clothes. When I got back to my things, somebody had swapped my new bloomers for an old washed out pair. They were blue just like mine and in my hurry to get dressed I didn't really notice, but Mama knew right away. Boy, was she mad! I had left home wearing nice new underpants and came back wearing some that were ready for the rag bag.

Seven

Sometimes I felt that things had always happened to me and none of it was good, but of course that wasn't true at all. One of the happiest days of my whole young life back then happened while I was still in first grade. Obviously, it had nothing to do at all with school. Rather, we were visiting with Tante Marie and her gang on Sunday as usual, when Mama mentioned that she was looking for a bigger doll for me as she thought Karin and I had outgrown our little baby dolls.

She already had one for Karin, a big jointed doll with a celluloid head, which may have belonged to Karola at one time. I'm not sure, but Mama would not give it to Karin until she had one for me too. She was fair minded that way. Neither one of us got anything, unless the other one got the same thing or something very similar, that way no one had to feel left out or cheated or jealous. She was a wise woman indeed!

While Mama was talking, my cousin Betty started rummaging around in an old chest of drawers, and next thing you know, she put the most beautiful doll I had ever seen in my arms for me to keep and take care of. She told me her name was "Gusti," short for Augustina, but I could name her something else if I wanted to. This was a doll Mama had given to Betty sixteen years earlier when Betty was only five years old and it is quite possible that Mama had this in the back of her mind all along.

Production of this kind of doll with its porcelain head, real human hair, eyes that closed when lying down and jointed arms and legs that bent in every direction, had ceased long ago, so one couldn't just go to the store and buy one. She was a big doll, and when standing next to me she came all the way up to my waist, but poor Gusti had seen better days and couldn't stand at all. All the elastic material that held her together on the inside had stretched out, making all her limbs dangle and her head bobble helplessly and her little feet were crumbling. She was actually quite pitiful, dressed in an old slip and a baby sweater that was too big on her.

But for me, it was absolute and unconditional love at first sight from the moment I saw her and I wouldn't have dreamed of changing her name, which somehow seemed to suit her perfectly. Proudly, I carried her home with her long, gangly legs slapping against mine, making walking quite difficult. Mama offered to carry her, but I just could not let go of her.

Next morning, I didn't want to go to school because I felt that Gusti needed me. But Mama promised to look after her while I was gone and made me go to school. Eventually I had to let Gusti go for a while though, to spend some time at the "Puppendoktor," the doll doctor, to get all her little hurts fixed. When I got her back, she was able to hold up her head and her limbs were tight and her feet were smooth and fixed. She didn't seem like the same doll anymore. Instead of the helpless bobbling baby, she was a little girl now, just like me and Mama even made her a blue pleated skirt just like mine and a blouse to match and she got some shoes and stockings, and underwear.

She seemed older and wiser, which of course she was older than I and I wasn't too sure about this transformation at first. But before long, she became my very sorely needed best friend and confidante. When Karin and I were fighting and Mama was yelling and Frl. Ewald was mean and it seemed like nobody loved me, there was Gusti with her sweet, kind understanding face listening to all my girlish woes and it all didn't seem so bad anymore.

Meanwhile, other good things were happening in our lives. The war of course was raging on and expanding all over Europe and far into Russia with no end in sight, but incredibly Papa was allowed to come home. In spite of the sparkling, brand new Autobahn, it was discovered that the most efficient and reliable mode of getting things and people from point A to point B was still the good old German railroad, and of course it took good, experienced people to operate it. Thanks to Dr. Strauss' urging for a job change years earlier, Papa had experience and therefore was given the chance to come home and just in time too.

Papa's role in the war had been mostly occupational in Poland, but soon after he left, his old unit—mostly other Wurzburgers of his same age group, were transferred to the Russian front. Very few, if any survived as they were either killed outright or captured by the Russians. It was wonderful having Papa back home and he had some fascinating stories to tell, not all of them meant for our little ears I am sure. One such story involved a scene he had come across while doing a house-to-house search, of a screaming young woman lying on a kitchen table trying to give birth, with her husband by her side to assist her and all the other young children standing around the table watching with great, big eyes.

It was hard to imagine people living in more primitive conditions than we did, but Papa was appalled at the filth and poverty he came across in some areas of Poland, where human beings and livestock lived together in one room shacks with dirt floors and thatched roofs, and no electricity, running water or toilet facilities at all. We didn't have electricity either, but at least we had running water in our kitchen, and a toilet that flushed downstairs.

Three of our four rooms had wooden floors, which Mama waxed and polished to a soft sheen. The kitchen had a stone floor, which was a lot more practical as it got soaked regularly when we took our Saturday evening bath. Mama used to bathe us in her little washtub, her "Wannle," until one day when Mama and Papa came home carrying a big standard size gray metal bathtub with a slanted side on one end. It required huge amounts of hot water, which Mama heated in her big wash pot and various other large pots on the kitchen stove, making the kitchen all steamy and cozy warm. Karin and I had a ball splashing around together in this big tub and sliding down the slanted end, like a big waterslide.

We had never heard of shampoo back then. Mama would just wash our hair with the soap powder she used for our fine washables, and rinse it with pitchers of fresh water. The last pitcher would have a good shot of vinegar in it to get out all the soap and make our hair shine. We loved the taste of vinegar running down our faces and we would lick our lips, until Mama told us to cut it out.

After our bath, we quickly had to go to bed, to give Karola some privacy for her bath. They would just scoop out some of the soapy water with a bucket and pour in more fresh, hot water, repeating this same process for Mama and then for Papa. He was always the last one, because he got the dirtiest, working at the railroad.

In the end, all the water had to be scooped out and poured down the sink and the tub was stored in the attic above us until next time. It was quite labor intensive, like everything else back then, and impossible for Mama to do without Papa's help. So while he was gone, we had to resume bathing in the little tub, which was no fun at all. This was just one of the many, many reasons we were so happy to have Papa back.

One thing we didn't like too much was when he cut our hair. He had a professional hair cutting kit with barber scissor, clippers and all and as soon as our hair started touching our shoulders a little bit, out came the kit and the cutting began. Karola's hair had some natural curl to it so it looked good short. But Karin's hair and mine was straight as an arrow and flat. We would beg him to at least leave our ears covered, which he was aiming to do, but by the time he got it even all the way around, there would be our earlobes hanging out bigger than life every time.

Mama tried to "pretty us up" by putting great big taffeta bows on top of our heads and we had them in all colors imaginable to match every outfit we owned. We thought they looked like airplane propellers that would make us fly away any minute, but Mama thought we looked adorable and she was so proud of us. At least we never got lice and Mama thought short hair prevented that and maybe she was right.

She would also cut our fingernails almost to the quick every time they got nice and long for scratching or digging, she said they collected too much dirt, which was nasty. It also prevented me from doing too much damage to poor Karin whenever I got mad and tried to scratch her. As we got older though, I didn't do that too much anymore.

I gradually came to terms with the fact that she was and always would be smarter than I, and more importantly, more level headed. Where I was rash and impulsive, she would think things through and consider the consequences first. That didn't always prevent her from doing crazy and potentially dangerous things though.

One way we amused ourselves while home alone, was to play hide and seek, coming up with ever more outlandish and unexpected places to hide in our small apartment. One time, after much searching I found her on top of the tall clothes closet, the "Kleiderschrank," squeezed in behind some boxes Mama stored up there. How she got up there is a complete mystery still because then she had trouble getting down from there.

Another time she had me completely baffled. I had looked absolutely everywhere I could think of, but she was nowhere to be found. The door was locked so I knew she had to be inside, but she wasn't. The only other escape would have been through the window, but we lived up on the third floor, a long way down to the ground, but something made me look out the bedroom window anyway.

Mama had made it a habit to only uncover one half of the double window to let in some light in the mornings, making it easier and quicker to cover it at night for blackout. And there was Karin crouching underneath the covered window on the steep, slick tile roof hanging onto the window-sill. She had been out there a long time and she was hot and tired and very upset with me because it took me so long to find her. And I was very upset with her for scaring me half to death.

I couldn't even breathe until she was safely back inside and I scolded her for doing such a crazy stunt. Of course long ago we had made a pact never to tell on each other, so my lips were sealed, but we both got in trouble over it anyway, Karin for doing it and I for not telling. All because Frau Heimbeck from up the street, whom we considered to be the neighborhood gossip, had seen Karin out on the roof and told Mama all about it.

Actually we had both been out on that roof before. Every once in a while something would sail straight out those wide open windows in summer and get caught on the snow fence which was attached to the edge of the roof, probably to keep avalanches of snow from sliding down on unsuspecting passersby in winter. If we couldn't retrieve or dislodge whatever was out there with a broom or yardstick, Papa would lift one of us out on the roof, holding on to one of our arms so we could reach down with the other one. It was kind of scary, but we knew Papa was holding us tightly and never would let us fall. He surely didn't mean to give Karin ideas for a new hiding place!

What flew out the window more than anything else were our ping pong balls, when we played ping pong on the big dining room table with the extra leaves put in and the net stretched across the middle. Those little celluloid balls just didn't always want to go where they were supposed to go. Sometimes they ended up with big dents in them, making them unusable, but Papa showed us how to hold a lighted match close to the dent and the heat would make the dent pop right back out. It was so neat to see this that we sometimes tried to make dents deliberately, but not too often.

We were raised to respect and take good care of everything we owned. We could play with anything we wanted to, but when done, we were expected to put things back the way we found them. Anything that came in a box, such as the ping pong set, had to be put back into the original box and put in its designated place. This was true of the little windup train set too, that Papa had bought for "the Child" when Karola was just a baby. He loved to help us setup the tracks and play with it, but when done, it had to go back into its original box with a spot for every car and it still looked new after all those years of playing.

We would let our little tiny doll house dolls ride on the train and in May when every kid in Germany including us had a shoe box with little holes punched in the lid, full of "Mai kafer," May bugs, they also got a ride on the train sometimes. These bugs or beetles, similar to a June bug only bigger and cuter, must be native to Germany or Europe, as I've never seen them in America. Their life cycle consists of several different stages, the one as a beetle being quite short-lived, only one month during the month of May.

So, early in May when they first started appearing, we would be out there on the prowl looking for them. They especially loved the horse chestnut trees of which Wurzburg had in abundance. One could always find some around there in the evenings when they were swarming. Since they weren't aerodynamically built and kind of clumsy, they would just smack into the tree trunks and fall down making it easy to pick them up.

Karola remembers going out in the woods with Papa real early in the mornings and shaking trees where they were sleeping and they would just fall out of the trees.I don't really remember doing that myself, though. But we had some every year, as did all our friends and neighbors.

We would line their boxes with fresh greenery and feed them lilac blossoms, which just happened to bloom in May and were another favorite of theirs. With their short little legs, black bellies with strips of white triangles on each side, hard brown wings which covered a set of tissue fine ones underneath and short feelers, which stuck out of the side of their heads, ell-shaped like antlers, they had an irresistible, clown-like quality. The tips of those antlers ended in little brushes, almost like eyelashes, the length of which determined if they were male or female, the longer ones being male.

The broad shield between their heads and wings told us what kind they were. Some had a shiny black one, and they of course were chimney sweeps, others with fuzzy white stuff on their shield were millers. The rarest and most prized ones had a reddish shield, and those were Emperors.

We would let them run races with each other, or build long tunnels out of dominos and let them crawl through there, closing one end off so they would crawl toward the light at the other end. And of course we gave them rides on the train or on our doll carousel. They couldn't fly away, unless they first pumped themselves up. So when they started pumping, it was time to put them back in the box.

Toward the end of May when they started acting really sluggish and weren't much fun anymore, we knew that this lifecycle was coming to an end, so we would just set the open box out on the windowsill and let them fly away to do whatever they did in their next cycle, some of which was spent underground. People loved these little critters so much that one can buy chocolate replicas in all different sizes of them just like chocolate bunnies or Santa Clauses.

Back then though, as the food supply got shorter and ever more tightly controlled, those kind of frivolous things gradually disappeared from the stores along with everything else that didn't grow in Germany and therefore had to be imported. A special treat for us was the banana Mama bought for us whenever we went to the marketplace. She would partially pull the skin down on all four sides for us and let us eat right there and then, and no banana since then has tasted as good as these did back then.

One time, when I was five years old, Mama and I had gone to the market without Karin, as she wanted to stay home with Papa. It must have been cold, because Mama was wearing her green overcoat with the fur collar. I got my customary banana and was thoroughly enjoying it while following Mama's green coat from market stand to market stand, taking in all the different sights and smells of all the fruits and vegetables and flowers and greenery that was for sale there. There were even crates with live geese, ducks and rabbits that one could buy.

There were a lot of interesting things to see as I kept on following this green overcoat. The trouble was, when I finally looked up at the person wearing it, it wasn't Mama at all. I had been following the wrong coat. Remembering the heroic tale of how Karola had found her way home when she got lost, which by then had been told many times, I decided the best thing to do was to go straight home, as I didn't think that I would be able to find Mama in this big, crowded market place.

To tell the truth, I didn't even try to find her. I felt scared and vulnerable by myself maybe stemming from the kidnapping years earlier. I didn't look left or right, I just wanted to go home. Papa was surprised to se me come home alone and for Mama, it was "deja vous," all over again and she was really angry with me, thinking I had gotten lost on purpose. In the end, I didn't get any praise at all for finding my way home by myself, only an angry tongue lashing. Soon after that, bananas completely disappeared from the market and it would be years before we ever ate another one, the taste of which became a fond and distant memory.

The same happened with Mama's rice pudding. No more rice was available, so that was the end of that. Real tea and real coffee had become a rarity, so people were drinking herbal teas, sweetened with saccharin because sugar was in short supply. Instead of grinding up real coffee beans in our wooden coffee grinder with the handle on top, which we loved to do because it filled the kitchen with a wonderful aroma, we now ground "spitzbohnen," pointed beans that weren't coffee beans at all, but roasted dark brown wheat kernels.

Somehow they just didn't have the same effect or flavor as real coffee, but that's what we mostly drank now. It was called ersatz coffee, which means substitute not the real thing and there were a lot of other ersatz things in our lives now. Milk was still milk but we got less and less of it and it was so thin that it looked blue. It was called "magermilch," which meant lean milk or skim milk, as all the fat had been taken out. It still had to be boiled as it wasn't pasteurized, but without the fat, it would badly scorch the pot every time and give this so-called milk a burnt taste.

Someone came up with the idea to melt a little butter in the pot first and that would prevent some of the scorching. It really worked, but of course butter was in short supply too. We would joke about how to stretch the butter by putting it on bread, smearing it all around and then scraping off more than we had put on in the first place. Bread of course was never eaten before it was several days old and dry because it was "more digestible" that way. It also went further that way because it could be sliced thinner.

But people coped and tried to find a little humor in every bad situation. When meat rations got scarcer and scarcer, cats were disappearing and people started calling them "roof rabbits," since they used to climb around the steep roofs all the time. Without their fur and tail, they looked very similar to rabbits. It is up to anyone's imagination what happened to all the cats in the neighborhood. A lot of people suddenly developed a taste for horsemeat, which was available without meat coupons at the horse butcher shop, close to the old Saints Bridge. We would see people lining up there sometimes when it was announced that they had a fresh supply.

But Mama thank goodness, was totally disgusted by that kind of thing and refused to even consider cooking something like that. She actually had a little trouble cooking the rabbits we got from Tante Marie, but she would soak them for a few days in a vinegar, onion and spices mixture and then boil them and chop them into pieces and put them in a brown sweet and sour gravy. That's as far as Mama went, cooking "exotic" things.

Chickens were only kept to lay eggs back then and when they got too old to do that, they ended up in the soup pot. The same happened with roosters. When they got old and cantankerous, or aggressive, they became chicken soup also. We never really had access to that kind of thing though, and I believe I was an adult by the time I ever tasted my first piece of chicken. I have to say, it tasted like rabbit to me.

Food wasn't the only thing that was strictly controlled and rationed. The same was true of just about every other necessity of living, such as coal for heating, gas for our light and cooking, soap for bathing and washing and any kind of blankets, linens, clothing and shoes. Everything we owned had to last seemingly forever, as it couldn't be replaced very easily.

Mama taught us how to darn our stockings, socks and underwear before the holes got too big and out of hand. That was our responsibility, as she wouldn't let us wear them with holes in them. She even found a way to extend the life of our bed sheets that had worn paper thin from use. She would cut them straight down the middle and sew the outside edges together. Since they had always been tucked under the mattress they were still in much better shape. She extended the lives of our towels that way too.

Nothing was ever just tossed out; even things that seemed beyond all hope Mama would still find some use for. Our friends and neighbors and family knew better than to throw anything out they didn't want anymore. Mama always gladly and gratefully accepted it. It became Karin's and my job to carefully take any piece of clothing apart at the seams, being careful not to cut into the material. We used razor sharp little pocketknives for that and sometimes we cut our fingers too.

Mama would wash and iron the pieces and roll them up to store them for future use. Her lady's magazine was full of great ideas and tips on how to make something new out of something old, or how to create a new dress or coat out of two old worn out ones. If the material got too shabby and faded on the outside, quite often it was possible to still use the inside. Even outgrown sweaters could be unraveled and the yarn used to make mittens, hats or socks, or it could be combined with something else to create a new sweater.

Everybody got really creative that way and of course there wasn't a girl in Germany that didn't know how to knit. It was required learning just like reading and writing. One thing Mama didn't trust herself to do was to repair Papa's shirts. She just didn't think she was talented enough. But there was a store in Wurzburg that specialized in doing that. They would use the long tail sections to make new collars and cuffs, to replace the old torn and frayed ones, which was mostly what got worn out. They would replace the tail section with some other material, but no one ever saw that anyway, and the shirts looked like new again.

Even though we were at war, people took great pride in their appearance back then. We had Sunday coats and dresses and some for weekdays, the Sunday ones being a little newer and dressier and we even wore dressy hats and gloves on Sunday, and it always made us feel special and we would try to act more lady-like. Actually, we could have done without the hats, which we thought looked even stupider than the propeller bows, but Mama was a very forceful woman and there was no use arguing with her. Her word was law at our house and Papa backed her up all the way, so we wore the stupid hats.

One big problem was shoes. They rationed and they were also very expensive, so we had to take good care of them as well. Saturday mornings Karin and I would have to gather up all the family shoes, scrape and brush all the dirt off, apply the appropriate color shoe polish to all of them, let the polish dry and then buff them to a high sheen. It kept us busy and out of trouble for a couple of hours anyway. Papa said leather needed food just like we did, and the shoe polish was that food for our leather shoes. He of course did his part by keeping them in good repair. The only problem was he couldn't make them bigger and children's feet have a nasty habit of growing.

Getting a new pair of shoes always stimulated my feet to grow a couple of inches immediately, or so it seemed. Nobody realized back then that all feet were not created equal, shoes that fit Karin just fine fell off my long skinny feet and it was extremely difficult to find some for me that were long enough but not too loose. We may have bought them a little bit too short for that very reason, but I didn't know that then. If they looked cute and they stayed on my feet and didn't hurt my toes while walking up and down the red carpet in the shoe store, they were considered a perfect fit.

But soon thereafter, on our long walks to Tante or wherever they would start hurting my toes terribly. It didn't do any good to go crying to Mama about it as it would only upset her and she couldn't go out and buy more shoes anyway. A big part of my childhood was spent walking around in terrible pain with my toes curled under, because my shoes were too small. One would think it would have at least stunted their growth a little bit, but that didn't happen either. As soon as I got new shoes they would make up for lost time and the whole cycle started over.

Sometimes my legs would hurt more than my feet from all the walking we did, especially coming home from Tante Marie's on Sunday evenings. But I wouldn't trade the memory of those walks for anything. Just being out after dark was exciting and sometimes it would be so pitch dark on that lonely road up on the hill that you couldn't see your hand in front of your face. But there would be our beautiful Wurzburg down below with its sparkling lights in the distance and the big sky above with its millions and millions of stars.

Papa would point out different constellations to us, like the Big Bear and the Big Dipper and Orion. Far off we would hear a nightingale make its hauntingly lonely, unforgettable sound, almost like a woman sobbing—just beautiful! And there would be crickets chirping and an occasional frog croaking. Sometimes the grassy ditches along the road were aglow with fireflies. Papa even caught some for us, so we could see what they looked like. But up close they weren't cute at all.

Sometimes the moon would light our way and when it was full it was so bright, almost like daylight. We liked that a lot, especially after we had blackout and the city down below looked like a black hole. But, moon or no moon, there would be the Milky Way in all its glory right above us and we could only wonder at the beauty and mystery of it all. Sometimes we would get real lucky and see a shooting star and then it was time to make a great big wish.

The shortest way home was to cut through the park called "Klein Niz-za," which looked especially lovely on a moonlit night with its long, curving duck pond and its weeping willow trees. But when it was dark, it was really, really dark. Mama would light the way with her little flashlight she always carried in her purse, but she could only use it sparingly as batteries were hard to come by also. We always had some sitting on the stove close to the stovepipe to warm them up and extend their lifespan somewhat.

Sometimes the beam of her flashlight would surprise some young lovers in the park, standing in a tight embrace clinging to each other, and Mama would quickly turn her flashlight off. We would just catch a quick glimpse of a uniform or some shining boots, since all young men were in the military by then. Even though there was a war, young people would meet, fall in love, spend some precious hours together and then have to say goodbye, quite often forever. But nobody dwelt on that, everybody was optimistic that this war would soon end and everything would be normal again.

Eight

It was on one of our visits to Tante Marie that we learned that our cousin Karola was getting married and of course we were all invited. As the youngest member of the whole clan, I was chosen to carry the bride's very long veil. That was customary back then and a great honor for me, and very exciting. Karin would be the youngest bridesmaid and Karola was also in the wedding party.

The date chosen was the Sunday after Easter, called "White Sunday" because that is the Sunday all Catholic children have their first communion with all the girls wearing white and as it happens, this was the year 1941 when Rudi had his first communion. So it was a double celebration. Such a big event of course called for some very special finery and everyone's sewing machine started humming and working overtime.

Karola, the bride who was very skilled at making all her own clothes including suits and overcoats, made her own wedding dress. Betty, her sister who of course was also in the wedding made a beautiful long dress for herself and one for her mother, Tante Marie. Hanni, Mama's youngest sister who was the same age as the bride, had recently ended a four-year relationship with the love of her life, a young man named Urban.

By accident she had found some love letters he had written to another girl, leaving her devastated, so she didn't want to go to the wedding at all. But everybody started talking to her until she relented and she also made a nice long dress for herself. It wasn't customary back then for all the wedding party to be dressed alike and it made for a pretty colorful picture, al these different beautiful long dresses. It also required a lot of hunting and scrounging to find the material and even sewing thread and notions.

But Mama persevered and found some beautiful silky light blue material, "Kunstseide," (artificial silk) enough to make Karin and me each a long dress with long puffy sleeves and big wide sashes that tied into a bow in the back. For our hair, she made hair bands out of the same material, so we didn't have to wear the "propeller bows." For Karola, she found some silky material with a white background and a flower pattern in pink, green and black—very sophisticated—creating a dress that made our Karola who was sixteen years old then appear all grown up.

I don't remember Mama ever making a dress for herself. She had her "good black dress" and that's what she wore, but she wanted us to look nice and she sure was proud of her girls. She also was everybody's favorite aunt and she had an especially close relationship with her niece Karola, who was often at odds with her own mother, Tante Marie.

It was almost instant "admiration society" the first time we met Arthur Schwartz, the future bridegroom. He was a member of the German Luftwaffe (air force) and he looked absolutely dashing in his blue uniform, tan and handsome with a beautiful smile, very friendly and outgoing, even talking to Karin and me, when most grown ups just ignored us. We could see right away why Karola fell in love with him and vice versa.

Karola herself was a beautiful girl with long, black, wavy hair and a beautiful smile and a sweet personality. Even though Tante Marie was a typical "Kemmer" and Uncle Willi Leopold had a swarthy, gypsy-like appearance, all their children turned out exceptionally good looking, with wavy curly hair, olive complexions, dark eyes and beautiful white teeth.

We don't know for sure how Karola and Arthur met, but it's pretty sure to assume that Arthur, being stationed at the Flugplatz, was at one time one of the guards walking the perimeter of the airfield. Tante knew them all and her little house and friendly face became a welcome sight to those young men on their lonely route with their dogs their only companion. She was always ready for them with a hot cup of coffee in winter or a nice cold glass of water in summer to be passed across the fence along with a few encouraging words.

When the long awaited big day finally arrived, it seems that they had invited Arthur's whole company. Not only were there enough escorts for all the young ladies, there were enough to line both sides of the aisle all the way to the altar. They stood facing the aisle in their fancy dress uniforms, with their knee high boots and flared at the hip pants, with their drawn sabers held high, forming a canopy for the wedding party to walk under.

German brides aren't "given away" by their father as is customary in America, instead the bride and groom come into the church together, walking down the aisle with their whole entourage following behind. So there we were, Karola and Arthur, both smiling and happy and looking absolutely gorgeous up front, me behind, carrying Karola's beautiful long veil and directly behind me, the youngest couple, Karin escorted by Rudi, both looking adorable with Rudi wearing his sailor suit from his first communion from earlier that morning.

The scent of lilacs and Easter lilies filled the air and along with all the flowers on the altar, there was a sea of candles burning. It was a regular fairy tale wedding, the kind every little girl dreams about. Afterwards there was a big feast and party at Tante's. The ladies must have been baking and cooking for days. Somebody had connections somewhere to come up with all this food. They were even roasting a goat, along with a lot of other things. Tante had no qualms about cooking "exotic" things at all, unlike Mama. From the sound of things and the few remaining snap shots, everyone had a wonderful time.

Unfortunately I was having one of my bouts with tonsillitis with chills and high fever. I barely made it through the ceremony. Mama stuck me in one of Tante's beds in one of her back bedrooms where I could hear the sounds of laughter, music and fun, but I was too sick to participate. This pretty well became the story of my younger years.

The only cure for infected tonsils in those days was heat and bed rest. The heat was supposed to help my body cook and destroy the invading and rapidly multiplying bacteria that was making me sick in the first place. Hot compresses didn't work too well, so Mama would put hot, boiled and crushed potatoes wrapped in a towel around my neck, because they stayed hot longer. But then, the heat and the battle going on inside my body made my fever soar.

I remember one time waking up in the middle of the night from a very fitful sleep feeling like my legs were running away and I couldn't stop them. My terrified cries must have roused the whole family. Karin later told me she saw my legs and my whole body twitching, apparently from a seizure. After it was finally over, I was totally spent and exhausted and I was terribly afraid that it would happen again and didn't want to go back to sleep anymore. It only happened one more time, several years later and then it wasn't quite as severe, but I lived in fear that this would happen again, every time I got sick, which was at least two or three times a year.

I don't think people understood back then the role aspirin could have in lowering one's temperature. They only thought it was good for headaches. Of course I couldn't have swallowed it anyway and there was no chewable baby aspirin or liquid or anything else, other than throat lozenges and they only made my throat hurt worse. It was a three-week ordeal every time for my body to kill off the bacteria. Three weeks of lying in bed, too sick to eat or even lift my head off my pillow, three weeks of no school.

When I was finally able to go back, I would be so lost, especially in math. I had no clue what they were doing. My best friend in school those first few years was Henrietta Solf, "Henny" for short. She was a sweet pretty girl, but she had the same problem with her tonsils as I did. Sometimes I would come back after three weeks and then she would be out for three weeks. So we didn't get to see each other very much and couldn't really help each other.

If it hadn't been for Karin, I probably would have flunked a few grades, but she would patiently explain to me what I had missed in school and what I didn't understand time and time again, and she would get me all caught up again. She was a straight-A student and a terrific teacher and, she didn't think so but she also had artistic abilities.

She was completely astonished when her drawing of an apple tree with all its intricate branches, twigs and leaves was chosen to be woven into a tapestry that was destined to be displayed in a museum for German modern art. Hitler, being an artist himself, wanted to encourage children to explore and use their different talents, which really wasn't done all that much until then.

One big hang up Karin had been writing essays. She just absolutely hated it and insisted she couldn't do it, to the point where she would sit there and cry in frustration. This of course broke my heart to see her so miserable, but I didn't know how to help her. I had no problem writing my own essays, which didn't always earn an "A," but I always liked writing and certainly didn't agonize about it. She would have to write about subjects I knew nothing about, so sympathy and encouragement was about all I could offer her, which didn't seem to help much.

Luckily, Papa loved to write and he always came to her rescue and more or less wrote her essays. He had a real flair for writing and even could put words together so they would rhyme, in other words he was a poet. One time he wrote a regular saga with many stanzas, all rhyming beautifully, an absolute masterpiece and Karin frankly admitted to the teacher that her father had written it. But the teacher was so impressed, that Karin got an "A" anyway and she was allowed to read it to the whole class.

Sometimes I wonder if the fact that she was left handed, but was forced to write with her right hand, somehow stifled her thought processes, because she was so brilliant in every other way. She also was fearless, or at least she put up a very brave front. When we saw a loose dog in the street and especially if he barked at us, I was extremely afraid, but she would protect me and look that dog straight in the eye, while we were walking by. Years later, she confessed that she was just as scared and shaking in her shoes while doing that.

One time she carried her bravery toward animals a little bit too far and it got the better of her. Just two houses down from where we lived, there was a guest house, sort of a corner pub on the bottom floor of a big four story apartment house where some of our friends lived. Almost every week, a wagon drawn by two big workhorses would deliver large barrels of beer or three foot long bars of ice for cooling the beer. It would take quite a while to unload these wagons, and probably it was interrupted by a little "beer break" every now and then.

Meanwhile the horses just patiently stood there hitched to the wagon, attracting lots of flies and neighborhood kids. The horses would stamp their hooves and swish their tails to get the flies off, and sometimes they would relieve themselves right there, astounding us kids with the sheer volume of their output.

Everybody kept a respectable distance from these big awe inspiring beasts until one day when Heini Bitter, a little wiry kid from the house next door got real brave and frisky and kept running over to the horses, touching them and running right back. Karin of course had to top this by standing very close to them and even sashaying right in front of their noses back and forth a few times.

One of the old, tired horses just finally had enough of this nonsense and grabbed the back of her sweater with his mouth and held her up in the air for awhile, just like a mother dog holds her pup by the scruff of the neck. When she started hollering "Mama," the horse released her and other than her hurt dignity, she was unharmed. She later acknowledged that she was showing off and probably needed to be taken down a notch and we laughed about this incident for years.

But I didn't think it was so funny when my own dignity took a bruising, sometime after that, and nobody laughed then. It was "Fronleichnam," the feast of Corpus Christi, celebrated annually on a Thursday in mid-June when the whole city shut down for this huge procession by the Catholic Church. The bishop in his golden robes would carry the "Monstranz," a vessel representing the body of Christ, accompanied by all the priests in Wurzburg and all the nuns.

All the city officials wearing sashes or golden chains, and all the different fraternities in their colorful uniforms with plumed hats and shining boots and sabers participated as well as several brass bands and people carrying relics of saints encased in glass cases and other people carrying statues. All the different trades were represented as well as the military. It was a huge thing that lasted several hours. There were altars set up throughout the city and the procession would stop at each one to celebrate a "mini-mass" or something like that.

It was more or less mandatory for all Catholic children to attend every year and we really didn't mind at all, even though it was very tiring. Little girls had the special honor of walking directly in front of the bishop and strew little flower buds on his path for Jesus. They would wear their prettiest white or pastel colored dresses with little wreaths of flowers in their hair, carrying baskets of flowers and looking cute as buttons, Karin and I included of course.

On this particular day, we were wearing our long, blue dresses, which were practically brand new still, since we had only worn them once to Karola's wedding. In the meantime, Mama had found some wreaths of pink and blue little flowers for our hair and we carried baskets of wild flowers that we had picked in the meadow down by the river. But we were late and we were running through this little street to catch up with the procession at one of the altars, when some runt of a Schnauzer shot out of one of the houses along the way and came straight for me and bit me in my tush. My worst nightmare had finally come true, but I have to say, it really didn't hurt that much. It was just a little nick, but it sure hurt my feelings and dignity and it made a little hole in my beautiful dress and all my flowers spilled out of my basket, but we went on to the procession anyway.

Actually, we got a lot more wear out of those lovely dresses than Mama could have ever imagined when she first made them. We wore them to two more weddings the following year and to countless other processions, mostly up at the "ReurerKirche." We belonged to St. Peter, the church directly across from our school, but the church closest to our house was the ReurerKirche, just up the street from us.

It was a very old church that belonged to a group of Franciscan monks. This church along with dorms and offices for the brothers filled up the whole block between Reurer Gasse and Sanderstrasse. One could enter the church from both streets, but we always used the Reurergasse entrance because it was closer to us.

These monks apparently loved the pomp and pageantry of a procession, especially during their evening service. Frequently, one of their faithful church workers, Frl. Leipold, would catch us on our way home from school and more or less beg us to come for the procession in the evening, always reminding us to be sure to wear our blue dresses.

She always managed to drum up a whole bunch of kids that way and we would make this grand entrance along with all the monks and priests and altar boys in their robes, carrying candles and incense and bells. It was quite a show and we loved it. Frl. Leipold would position all of us girls on each side of the altar, making sure Karin and I would be in the most visible spot, right up front. All the while the organ would be playing up in the loft filling every inch of that church with incredible, beautiful music and then the ritual of the holy Mass would begin, all in Latin of course, making it that much more stirring and mysterious to us.

Actually, some of that mystery was unraveled for us during the year before our First Communion. We had to learn all the steps and their meaning of the Catholic Mass along with our catechism and all the creeds and prayers and the rosary. The priest taught us all this during religion class in public school. Lutheran children had to go to another room during this period where they learned religion from a Lutheran pastor. This made any kind of Sunday school or Bible school unnecessary and was not offered at all in Germany.

Karin's First Communion was in 1942, with mine following right behind the next year.

But Mama could see how bad things were getting by then and knew that they would only get worse where food was concerned for the party, or material for clothing and all the other supplies, such as white stockings, shoes, gloves, wreaths for our hair and even the songbook for church that children carried with a lace handkerchief. Someone suggested that we just get all those things for Karin and then I could use them the following year. But Mama wouldn't hear of it or consider it even for a minute.

Instead, she talked to the priest about letting me take my First Communion along with Karin. It so happened that there were three other children with this same request, so we got private lessons after school to prepare us for this important event. And Mama had a lot of preparing to do as well, just to find all the things we needed and then she had to make two of everything and of course it all had to be extra nice for our special day.

Like so many holidays in Germany, such as Easter, Christmas, Pentecost and others, Communion was a two-day affair. The first day was all about the church and being with all the family and close friends, eating and celebrating and then going back to church in the evening. The second day was spent outside, talking a long walk to some exciting destination, having refreshments and then coming back home—sort of a day trip on foot.

Some kids wore their Communion dress the second day, but a lot of them, including us, had a special "second day" dress that was worn with the long white stockings and the white wreaths in our hair. Our dresses were a soft red with little white collars and cuffs. Later these dresses became our Sunday dresses and we wore them with red or white propeller bows in our hair.

I don't think Mama ever slept during this time, as she did most of her sewing at night after we went to bed. Besides the red dresses and our white Communion dresses, she also made white overcoats for us, because traditionally from way back, "White Sunday" always was sunny but cold and the thin dresses alone wouldn't be warm enough.

We were so caught up in the preparation for our big day that we almost didn't have time to get ready for another big day, when our cousin Betty married Max Legemann a few weeks before our Communion. By then our blue dresses had gotten a little short on us and we had outgrown our white shoes so we had to wear black ones, which we didn't like. Papa was actually working on making our white shoes bigger so we could wear them for our Communion. Since they were made of cloth, he could put new toes in the front and make bigger bottoms so they fit again, but they weren't ready in time for the wedding.

Like Karola, Betty had made her own beautiful lace dress and she had a really long veil—eighteen feet long—and I of course was the designated veil bearer, but this one was so long and heavy that I couldn't do it by myself. Karin and Rudy had to help carry it. So we put Rudi in the middle and Karin and me on each side, strutting down the aisle together behind the lovely couple.

Betty was proudly carrying a big bouquet of white lilacs tied with silk ribbons, which according to German tradition, her bridegroom had presented her with just before the wedding. Actually, we had custody of this bouquet over night and I remember how Mama fretted over those flowers.

Our kitchen was too warm, so she put them in the attic, then she realized that we had frost that night, so she climbed up into the attic in the middle of the night to check and make sure that the lilacs weren't freezing. Happily they survived the night just fine and it was a lovely wedding, just not quite as big as Karola's though.

Max was a member of the Luftwaffe also, but he was with a different outfit than Arthur and he was more quiet and reserved and I believe he was higher ranking. There were fewer people at this wedding and no canopy of sabers to walk under. Immediately following the ceremony we had a date at the photographers for the official wedding pictures, another German tradition, but no other pictures exist of the party afterwards and I have no memory of it at all strangely enough even though I wasn't sick at the time.

We didn't really get to know Max that well, but he seemed to be a real gentleman. Unfortunately, his outfit was transferred soon after the wedding and we never saw him again after that. Betty never got to establish any kind of home with him or live together like husband and wife. The war and the different locations of his assignments made that impossible. A few short visits were all they ever had together and that ended when Max was sent to Russia.

They did create a beautiful little boy, though, whom they named Peter, the big fashion name of that era. We called him "Peterle," just a sweeter version of that name. There were actually songs written about "Peterle" and the name was very fitting. He was just about the cutest thing we had ever seen.

For me, his birth finally ended the seemingly unending "curse" of being the baby of the family. This was kind of a double edged sword for me as the attention was nice, but nobody ever thought anything I had to say had any kind of substance or importance—probably true! Of course, that didn't change at all, but at least everybody had a new focal point now.

But long before that, Karin and I had our First Communion, which turned out very, very nice. I never thought that we could fit that many people into our living room for the big sit down dinner. We must have borrowed chairs from the whole neighborhood or maybe they came from the guesthouse down the street, along with extra tables. And somebody must have brought extra china. Everything looked beautiful with white tablecloths and flowers everywhere.

While the whole family was at church and afterwards at the photographers, Tante Marie and her good friend Leni were at home in our kitchen cooking up a storm and they really outdid themselves. Everything was delicious as were all the different cakes Mama had baked and the beautifully decorated torte from the bakery. On our second day we visited the "Kappele," the pilgrimage church up on the hill across the Main River and one of the most beautiful and most photographed points in Wurzburg.

From there we went on to the "Frankenwarte," with its look-out tower and restaurant, a good walk past the Kappele through the woods, mostly uphill. This place actually had the only playground in Wurzburg at that time, just a few swings and some seesaws, and it was really popular and usually very crowded, but we got a little "swinging time" in too. It was a wonderful Communion and I will treasure the memory of those two days forever and ever. And then it was time for another wedding!

Hanni, our aunt who didn't even want to go to Karola's wedding actually met her future husband there. He was a friend of Arthur's, also in the Luftwaffe of course, and tall, blond and handsome. He was Hanni's escort at the wedding, as fate would have it, and soon romance was in the air for them. It was just what Hanni needed at that time.

The young man, Urban whom she had loved so deeply and who betrayed her, was killed in Russia, so there was no hope at all of any reconciliation. So sometime in the summer of 1942, Wilhelm Schaller became our new uncle, and we called him "Helm" for short. I, of course, had to carry Hanni's veil and I was becoming a real pro at this.

Mama in the meantime had time to catch her breath and figure out how to make our blue dresses longer, without having any extra material. Something inspired her to simply use the sashes and insert them between the tops and the skirts and they looked beautiful again. The shoes Papa had made bigger still fit, so we were all set.

The wedding feast this time was at our Oma and Opa's apartment on Domstrasse. Again, Leni was there to help with the cooking, just as she had done at the other two weddings and at our communion. She was somewhat of a tragic figure whose whole life was filled with pain and sorrow. She was forever wearing black as women in mourning do for a year after losing a loved one. But she was such a true blue friend who would have done just about anything in the world for us. We were so lucky to have her in our lives.

She was actually caught in one of the snapshots at Hanni's wedding when she was normally shy and tried to hide from the camera. And happily, I wasn't sick at this wedding, so I'm in some of those snapshots too along with Karin and Rudi and a whole lot of other people. Cameras didn't have flash attachments then, so they only worked outdoors, but we never owned one at all. I don't know who took those pictures.

Nine

The whole time all these wedding and communion plans were being discussed and preparations being worked on—mostly women's stuff—and affairs being celebrated, Papa was working on some plans of his own. As an employee of the German railroad, he was entitled to free travel for all of us, anywhere within the German borders, which now also included Austria all the way down to northern Italy. The war was being fought far outside the border still, and things were relatively calm and travel was considered safe, so Papa thought we ought to take advantage of our free tickets and have a family vacation.

Of course, even if the train was free, lodging, food, attractions and travel in the cities was not and that worried Mama. Papa assured her that he had pinched his pennies pretty hard and that he had saved up enough. There were no credit cards then. Everything was pay as you go, or don't go, but on the plus side, nobody had any debts then either. Family finances were still somewhat of a sore point for Mama. While Papa was in Poland, she had control of them and she felt that she had proved to him (and to herself) that she was trustworthy and responsible and could handle money very well.

But once he was back, everything went back to the old system where Mama got her weekly household money and Papa controlled the rest. She was completely in the dark about where they stood financially. That was Papa's secret. But at least she knew that he was very frugal and completely unselfish, never spending any big money just on himself. Of course she was exactly the same way. Everything was done or spent for the good of the family.

Actually, when Tante Marie learned of our vacation plans, she offered to keep us kids, so Mama and Papa could go alone, but neither one would hear of it. We would all go or nobody would go. So, once it was established that there was enough money, out came the big atlas and the plotting began. We always planned several routes and destinations, which Papa submitted to the railroad for approval, in order of preference, but it didn't really matter if we got first or third choice. They were all beautiful places.

The ocean never held any great attraction for Papa and neither did the hustle and bustle of the big cities of northern Germany. His great love was the beauty and serenity of the mountains of southern Germany—the Alps. So that's where we headed every year. That doesn't mean however that we avoided big cities altogether. Our jumping off point was always Munich or "Munchen" as we called it, which certainly qualifies as a big city even though it didn't feel that way, with its friendly, slow talking people and its laid back, easy going character.

Before we ever packed our first suitcase however, Mama would work herself into a frazzle, making some new clothes for us to wear on our trip. She wanted us to have at least one new outfit, possibly more to wear. For school, we would wear the same dress all week long, as was the custom back then. But when we traveled, Mama would have us alternate between outfits, to let the wrinkles hang out between wearing. It always cost her a few sleepless nights to get everything done and then there was the added worry that I might get sick at the last minute and mess up all our well-laid plans. Luckily, that never happened, but there were some pretty close calls once or twice.

For a family of five, we actually traveled pretty lightly. I remember one suitcase for the whole family, possibly two later, but by today's standards they were both pretty small. That was an absolute necessity since we had to "schlep" everything considerable distances quite often.

It started on what I like to call "DD Day," or day of departure, when we caught the early morning "schnellzug" (fast train) to Munchen. Usually we walked to the train station, which was at least twice as far as the marketplace. I don't know if it was too early for the streetcar to run, or if Papa thought the exercise would do us good, since we would be sitting on the train for four hours.

Of course, once we were on the train, there wasn't much sitting for Karin and me. We loved to get out from under Mama and Papa's watchful eyes and go exploring a little bit. It would have been terribly boring to just sit in the cabin, even though they were nice cabins, soft upholstered seats and all. The long hallway outside the cabins was a far more exciting place for us. One could even go from car to car through open-air connecting bridges, which was a little scary but that didn't stop us.

Wherever we went, restaurants or whatever, Karin always had to find out right away where the restrooms were located, with me just one step behind, of course, and the train was no exception. Much to our amazement, we discovered there that the toilet had a hole in the bottom, where one could observe the ground whizzing by underneath the train. Papa assured us that it was perfectly all right to use it that way, leading us to the conclusion that railroad tracks had to be nasty, disgusting places. I'm greatly relieved to know that all that has been changed since then.

Once we arrived at our destination, the first order of the day was to head for the Tourist Information Office, usually in the train station or next to it, to find affordable lodging for the night—preferably within walking distance to the station, or at least close to a streetcar or bus line. There was no such thing as Ramada Inns or Super8 Motels back then. Modern hotel and motel chains didn't exist in Germany then. We mostly stayed in privately owned "pensions," somewhat like a very basic, Spartan bed and breakfast inn. Or we stayed in small mom-and-pop hotels with the same type set-up.

One time, I forget where, but I think it might have been Innsbruck, there must have been some big, important event going on, so everything was filled up. We were stranded and more or less homeless in a big strange town—not a good feeling! Somebody suggested that we try the youth hostel a block or two away, so we raced over there and secured the last two beds on the women's side, which the four of us girls had to share. Papa had to sleep on the men's side where girls weren't allowed. I guess (and hope) he had a bed to himself there.

The beds were actually more like cots, and I remember rows and rows of them with only a little rack or nightstand between them. It was very, very close quarters indeed, and not exactly Mama's cup of tea. But for us kids, it was just another big adventure and it definitely beat sleeping under the stars in the cold, damp night air of Germany.

Another time we came extremely close to doing that very thing, though. This happened in the beautiful Bavarian town of Garmisch, where there was not one room to be had anywhere in the whole area. Some well-meaning helpful soul told us about an old farmhouse that had been turned into an inn with a restaurant about eight kilometers (5 miles) away, feeling fairly sure that there would be rooms available there because of the distance.

One could only get there by foot via a trail that went through the famous "Partnachklamm," an absolute must-see in Garmisch and this had been on Papa's list of things to do and see all along. This is where the river Partnach comes tumbling down out of the mountains squeezing through an incredibly narrow gorge (or klamm) where two mountains nearly touch each other for quite a stretch, creating this really wild, rushing, white-capped stream of water.

The trail runs along the very edge of one of the mountains, often running just inches above the wild water with just a thin metal guardrail for protection. A large section of the trail is overhung by a large section of the mountain above, giving one the feeling of walking through a cave, or tunnel. It is just an awesome place, to say the least, and very exciting. We had stowed most of our baggage at the train station, after putting just a few necessities into Papa's big brown canvas rucksack or backpack that we used to carry everywhere.

Mama always carried a bag with things for us to eat, because we would get really hungry from all that hiking. Usually it was a loaf of rye bread from the bakery and a knife to cut it with, a tin with butter and where available, we would stop at the market for some fresh fruit and sometimes we got some lunch meat at the butcher shop or cheese at the dairy. There were no supermarkets back then, where you could buy all these things in one place.

For thirst, Mama had a bag of hard candy for us to suck on. We really weren't used to drinking a lot and we never drank anything during meals at all. The thinking was that it was bad for digestion because it diluted the stomach juices. It's probably a miracle that we didn't all die of dehydration. What may have saved us were Germany's many, many fountains. Some were quite old, ornate and beautiful, while others were more utilitarian and very plain. All had perfectly good, drinkable water for thirsty people and animals.

We came across such a fountain on our way to the inn—a very plain one with a trough for cattle to drink out of, next to a huge meadow with tall grass ready for mowing to make hay for the winter. Scattered throughout the meadow we noticed several quaint wooden houses, called "Heustadl," or hay barns, which is where the hay was stored until needed.

The cows who would eventually be eating all this hay, meanwhile were high up on the mountain from Spring to Fall grazing the lush Alpine meadows called "alms," guarded by one person, a "sennerin," or cow herder—usually a young woman. Each cow wore a bell around its neck, making it easier to find if it strayed. Many romantic books and songs have been written about this lifestyle. This is where yodeling was born as a means of communications, where "senneris" would yodel to each other on the distant "alms," probably out of sheer loneliness.

The trail we were on may have led to such a place. It was mostly uphill and seemingly endless, but we never made it that far. Actually, we didn't even go as far as the inn, as we met some hikers coming back from there who told us that it was still quite a distance away and it was completely filled up. By then we were high up on a mountain ridge, with a deep canyon beside us, and another wall of mountains looming directly across. With Papa's opera glasses, we could make out climbers scaling that wall across the canyon and one could yell across there and it would come echoing back.

Thrilling as all that was, it didn't solve the problem of where we would sleep that night, however. We knew that once the sun went down, it would get dark and cold very quickly in the thin mountain air and we definitely didn't want to be caught up on that ridge after dark. The only logical thing to do was to head back toward town, a long way back.

It was dusk when we reached the meadow with the watering trough and the lovely "heustadl" filled with soft, fragrant hay and that's where we decided to spend the night. More than likely we broke some laws doing that since so many things were forbidden back then in Germany. I remember having to be very, very quiet as Papa was peering through the cracks in the wall at some passersby, worried that we might be discovered, evicted and punished or worse. Nothing like that happened though and this episode became one of our fondest memories that we talked and laughed about for years.

There were no theme parks back then, or anything remotely like that, so our vacations consisted mainly of sightseeing and looking up at things and Papa managed to make it fun and educational at the same time, most of the time. One of the first places we ever visited in Munich was a huge museum that must have covered a whole city block. We wandered for hours through room after room filled with wonderful treasures and artifacts from all corners of the earth, but when we came to a large hall full of paintings and statues of mostly nude men and women, Mama herded us out of there pretty quickly. It was considered unchaste to look at things like that.

Besides museums, Papa loved old churches and cathedrals which are so plentiful in Germany and we visited at least one in every town and city, not so much as worshippers, but to sight see and we learned a lot along the way. Papa taught us to really open our eyes and see the beauty of things all around us and appreciate the hard work and artistry that went into creating these things. Amazingly, he usually even knew what famous painter painted those beautiful frescos high up on the ceiling and walls we were gazing at, or what artist carved those intricate details on that altar, or who created those huge, wonderful stained glass windows, all of it done hundreds of years before we were born, and yet it was still fresh and new looking.

We learned to tell the difference between baroque and gothic style churches and a lot of the history along with it, but I have to admit, some of it was probably lost on our young minds. One of my most vivid memories stems not from what we saw inside the cathedrals, but what happened right outside one time. I can't remember what town we were in, but the church was probably gothic with its tall, pointed portals and its wide stairs leading down to a big plaza in front of the church.

As we were coming out of the dark church into the broad daylight, Mama noticed that a big moth or candle bug had landed on the back of Karin's collar and she approached Karin to get it off. But when Karin heard "bug," she let out some loud shrieks and literally flew down those stairs running around the plaza with her arms flapping like a giant bat, trying to shake her coat off, which was firmly attached at the wrists and wasn't about to budge. Mama always put tight bands at the end of our sleeves to keep the cold wind out, so they had to be unbuttoned first. We hated to hurt poor Karin's feelings, but it was so funny, we all laughed until we had tears in our eyes and she later had to laugh about it herself. Mama was just glad that she didn't see that bug inside the very quiet, solemn church, as there was no telling what would have happened.

One big attraction in Munich is the famous "Glockenspiel," at the Rathaus (city hall), where throngs of people gather at certain times of the day to watch larger than life-sized animated figures dressed in period costumes re-enact some important historical event while the bells are playing a pretty tune. This takes place in an opening in the building about three or four stories up. It is very interesting, entertaining and—best of all—it is free!

So here we were all standing there gawking up at the unfolding spectacle, when suddenly a big rainstorm came up, sending everyone running for cover and, as luck would have it, the cover we ran to just happened to be a movie house. Back then theaters had only one screen and they showed only one movie, but in big cities they showed that movie over and over around the clock, along with news clips and short features. The lights never came on. One could enter at any point and then stay as long as one wanted to. We thought that was pretty neat. Wurzburg didn't have anything like that at all.

The movie we saw that day had the unforgettable title, "Lump-batzivagabundus," a dark comedy about a charming hobo, filmed in black and white of course, as Technicolor movies were extremely rare back then. It didn't make any sense at all to me, but it was a thrill to be in a movie anyway. I thought the fact that we came in at the middle and saw the end before the beginning probably added to my confusion, plus I was still pretty young then. But many years later I saw that same movie from beginning to end and it still didn't make any sense to me—it must have been the movie!

Papa always said, Amerika made the best movies. He especially loved the hair-raising antics of Harold Lloyd and the sweet and sad silent comedy of Charlie Chaplin. We kind of suspected that Papa's little moustache was a tribute to Charlie Chaplin. He never would admit it though. Mama and Papa both also adored Shirley Temple movies and they even had chewing gum at the movies when they were young. But that disappeared along with all the foreign movies in Nazi Germany. We never got tired of listening to Mama and Papa telling us about these things though. I honestly can't say that we ever got bored on our trips, but there were some things that were even more memorable and fun than others.

One real high point for all of us was our visit to the zoo in Helabrunn near Munich, where we saw animals that we had only seen or read about in books and some we had never even heard about at all, in a beautiful open park-like natural setting. One huge attraction there, among so many other things, was a brand new baby elephant, one of the first ones ever born in a zoo and we learned that it takes almost two years for a baby elephant to grow in its mother's tummy—a staggering amount of time in a child's life.

So even when we thought we were just simply having fun, we were learning new things all the time too. We went from the very bowels of the earth where we watched salt being mined deep in a mine at Bad Reichenhall, to the very top of a very tall mountain near Innsbruck, named Hafelkar, a very strange name. We got there by means of a cable car, another tremendous thrill for us kids. For once, we were looking down on things instead of looking up all the time. The cable car ended at a building just below the summit, but it was an easy walk to the top except the air was thin up there and the wind was fierce.

I remember standing on top of Hafelekar gasping for breath, as everyone had told me to breathe through my nose, so the cold wind wouldn't get to my tonsils and make me sick, but I just couldn't get enough air through my nose. We didn't spend a whole lot of time on the mountain, the thrill was getting up there and getting back down in that little compartment hanging on a cable, and seeing snow even though it was summer, and going through a layer of clouds and also looking at Italy, but that only looked like more mountains to me.

One time we actually did take a little local train down to Villach, a border town where we saw Italian soldiers guarding the border and of course on the other side of the border there was Italy. We weren't allowed to go there, though German people have a special fascination for foreign countries and we certainly were no exception. Of course, since Innsbruck is in Austria, technically we were in a foreign country already, but since Hitler had brought Austria "home into the Reich," we considered it to be German, just like Bavaria or Prussia.

We did notice certain differences in the way people dressed or talked, or the way food was prepared or houses were built, but that was true of all different regions in Germany. Every area has its own dialect for instance. It's German, but it is pronounced in different ways and some of it is pretty hard to understand, especially for a foreigner. But we got a real kick out of listening to some of those people talking—and vice versa probably.

Another thing we noticed in Tirol, the area around Innsbruck, was the many elderly men and women with goiters—big fist sized lumps hanging on their necks which looked very unusual. Of course we weren't allowed to stare at them, we knew better than that and eventually we learned that it was a lack of iodine in their diet that caused that condition. The explanation was that the main source of iodine was fish from the ocean—in our case, the North Sea—which, as good Catholics, we ate most every Friday. In the Alps, being so far from any ocean, people ate mostly fish from the mountain lakes and streams and those fish have little or no iodine.

True or not, it made sense to us back then, and it helped us to eat our fish even if we didn't like it. Now, we can buy salt with added iodine and no one has to worry about getting a goiter on his neck, even people who hate fish of any kind and never eat it. I don't think that was available back then.

One of the most notable things we saw in Innsbruck (besides goiters) was a house with a roof made of gold, the "golden Dachl." We were really impressed by that! And I'm sure there was an interesting story connected to that too, but it escapes me at the moment.

What none of us ever forgot was our second excursion to a mountain top, the "Patscherkofel," by name. This one also had a cable car running to the top, but unlike Hafelekar, one could actually walk up there by way of a very steep, serpentine path snaking back and forth up the side of the mountain. This was some distance outside of Innsbruck. To get there we took a cog-wheel train, a completely different system than the coal-powered trains we were used to, and of special interest to Papa, the railroad man.

Of course, Papa loved to walk so the plan was to hike up the mountain, get some food and refreshments there, look around some and then take the cable car and the cogwheel train down and back to Innsbruck. The trek up the mountain took a lot longer than anticipated and it was late afternoon by the time we finally made it, and just as we were coming around the last bend we saw a cable car heading down the mountain.

But that didn't really concern us at the moment. Our mind right then was on getting something to eat and then getting a good look at the view around us before nightfall. Then we learned that the restaurant and everything else was closed because the whole crew had just caught the last cable car down—the last one of the day. So, even though we were hungry and tired, we had no choice but to walk back down the mountain, which was actually more difficult due to the steep grade.

Mama, whose feet were hurting badly, was so upset and she blamed it all on Papa. I don't really remember who walked with whom that beautiful moon-lit night, but Papa was way ahead with one or two of us girls and the rest were lagging behind with Mama, but Mama could be hard all over the mountain yelling and fussing and complaining all the way down. If there were any wild animals around, we surely didn't have to worry. I'm sure she scared them all away.

When we got back to the train station, we discovered that the train stopped running after the last cable car came down off the mountain, and of course it was long gone too. So, now we had to walk all the way back to Innsbruck. It was two o'clock in the morning when we reached our hotel and then we were locked out, of course. We had to bang and bang on the door to wake up the owner to let us in.

We were all starving, but aside from some sugar, there wasn't a crumb of food in our hotel room. Mama fixed us some sugar water to drink so our growling stomachs wouldn't keep us awake. As tired as we were, there wasn't much danger of that though. We didn't do much the next day, as everybody was so sore from all that walking, especially Mama and Papa. It hurt just to get up and down the sidewalk, or to sit down on a park bench or get back up from there.

In time, Mama forgave Papa and as the soreness faded away this became another memory to cherish and laugh about for years to come. It seems that we were in Innsbruck two years in a row, not only because it was a beautiful place, but also because that's what the railroad had approved.

One year we traveled from Innsbruck to Lindan am Bodensee (or Lake Constance as it is called on some maps), one of the most beautiful, breathtaking, unforgettable train rides ever. We went through and around and over the Alps, where every bend of the track brought another picture postcard view and quite often, another tunnel. Karin and I just loved to stand by the open window, drinking in the spectacular sights and letting the wind blow our hair and sometimes waving to people way down in a valley with a big white handkerchief, so they could see us better. And quite often they actually waved back, also with a handkerchief. What a thrill!

But trains were powered with coal back then and they were pretty sooty and dirty. Sometimes we would get a piece of dirt or soot in our eye, which really hurt and then we'd go crying to Mama, who had warned us all along that something like that would happen. It never deterred us for very long though.

I don't remember a whole lot about Lindan itself; apparently for once nothing really memorable happened to us there, or at least not much. One thing we learned there was that traces of some of the earliest human settlements in Europe, dating back to the Stone Ages, were found there at the Bodensee. Some ancient people had actually built a community on the lake, by driving heavy wooden pillars into the lake bottom and building their huts on connecting planks, probably to be safe from marauding tribes and wild animals. One could still see remnants of this ancient settlement and marvel at the ingenuity of these, our early ancestors.

The lake itself was, of course, the biggest body of water we had ever seen and I remember boarding the biggest ship I had ever seen for a sight-seeing trip, but the sights we saw were mostly water and kind of boring to us, so we explored the ship instead. We learned that on the other side of the lake was Switzerland, but one couldn't see the other side because the lake was too big. Even though the ship went way out, we never came close enough to take a good look at Switzerland. I don't think we even saw its shoreline.

For years after that, this is what we pictured the ocean was like, only bigger of course. But I have to say when I finally did see the real thing many, many years later when I was a young woman, it was totally overwhelming and nothing at all like the Bodensee or what I had imagined.

One place that was forever on our wish list of places to visit was Vienna, the city where so much of the world's most beautiful music was written by some of the world's most famous composers. We especially loved all those Viennese waltzes that Papa was teaching us to dance to and all those countless songs that were not only written in Vienna, but about Vienna, describing a lifestyle and atmosphere one could find nowhere else on earth. One famous song called it "Die Stadt Meiner Traume," (the city of my dreams) with its blue Danube River and its Vienna woods and narrow little streets with charming coffee shops or little wine restaurants with "Schrammel" music, a style of music only heard in Vienna, with violins and accordions—the sweetest sound this side of heaven.

There were so many, many other things we wanted to see there, but the railroad never approved a trip to Vienna, so it forever remained a dream for Karin and me to see this wonderful place. Even as we became two little old ladies, we were still dreaming to go there someday. One place they did approve was Salzburg, which is actually where Mozart was born and we got to see his birthplace and early childhood home, which really seemed quite modest to us.

As everyone knows, Mozart was a "wunderkind," or child protégé who composed and played beautiful music at the tender age of three already, charming and mesmerizing not only the whole royal court of Vienna, but royalty all over Europe, with his great talent and pleasing personality. The thing that stands out most in my memory of our visit to Salzburg was a totally enchanting puppet show with exquisitely dressed marionettes—ladies in their hoop skirts and men in silk britches, with elaborate powdered wigs and lots of ruffles, acting out little Mozart's visit with the Kaiser and his entourage. It was so well done and looked so real to us; we never even saw the many, many wires that controlled every single movement of those puppets. They looked like real people to us.

We knew that Mozart was a musical genius who wrote an incredible amount of beautiful music during his short life, his most famous and beloved composition probably being, "Eine Kleine Nachtmusik." Everybody knew that one. To this day, and as far back as I can remember, Wurzburg has celebrated an annual "Mozart fest," a one or two week festival every summer, completely dedicated to the music of Mozart with nightly performances in the gorgeous "Kaisersaal," in the Residenz or on warm summer nights, in the beautiful formal garden, the "Hofgarten," next to the Residenz.

Tickets for these events were pretty well out of our reach way back then, but we loved to hang out and watch the people streaming there from all directions in their formal evening wear, hoping that someday we could be part of that crowd. Then one time someone gave us some tickets for an afternoon performance in the Hofgarten, so we got all dressed up for that and had a wonderful time, strolling through the garden and listening to the strands of "Eine Kleine Nachtmusik" and other Mozart songs.

It seems that Wurzburg's love affair with Mozart was not entirely one sided. Apparently, Mozart's many travels had brought him to Wurzburg at least one time where he wrote a letter to his beloved wife Constance about the "beautiful, gorgeous town of Wurzburg." This was just one year before his untimely death in 1791 at age 33. We old Wurzburgers are very proud of that letter! There were a few summers, during the darkest hours of World War II and immediately afterwards that our Mozart fest had to be suspended, but that was only temporary, a few years at most.

Ten

What completely surprised me was the fact that Karola, my big sister, has no memory at all of our trip to Salzburg, even though she remembers all the details of our other trips and probably even better than I. The explanation of course was that she didn't get to go on this trip, a fact that I had forgotten. This must have been the year 1943 when Karola was drafted into the Arbeitsdienst at the age of 18.

All of a sudden, our Karola was all grown up and looking really sharp in her uniform. Her apprenticeship at the grocery store had taken a detour when the owner of the store, her boss, was drafted into the military and his young, pregnant wife was unable to keep things going and had to close the store. Luckily, Karola found another store by the name of Greib that was willing to take her on and let her finish her training.

She passed all the required exams with flying colors and became a full-fledged "verkauferin" with all the accompanying prestige and somewhat better pay too, but then the Arbeitsdienst called and her life took a different turn again. I don't know how she felt about it, but I know Mama wasn't ready for this. To her, Karola was still her little girl whom she wanted to protect and watch over at all cost.

Mama felt a little better after we were able to visit Karola at the camp where she was stationed, about a two-hour train ride from Wurzburg. It was actually a very nice camp in the middle of a wonderful smelling pine forest. We saw the barracks where she and probably a hundred or more other girls slept and it reminded us a lot of the youth hostel, where we had slept on one of our trips. We learned where they showered and where they ate, and it all seemed almost like fun.

But the discipline was very harsh and the work even harder. These girls were not there to have fun. Their main duty was to work the vast fields surrounding them and assist with all the farm work and livestock in the nearby villages. This was work most of them had never done, but it was sorely needed, since most of the men were now drafted and engaged in the war effort. Somebody had to grow food for the "Bevolkerung," (the people).

For most of these girls, Karola included, this was also the first time they had been away from home for any length of time and I am sure that homesickness was a big factor in their lives also. One couldn't even just pick up the phone and call home when things got tough, because nobody had a phone back then. The only means of communication was the mail or in a real emergency one could send a telegram, but that was very expensive and rarely done.

Actually, we did have an emergency that almost cost us our lives, while Karola was away, but it turned out okay, so no one sent a telegram then either. I still don't understand why nobody else smelled it, but I knew something smelled awful in the bedroom, much like powerful Limburger cheese and I told Mama about it. But she thought it was just a delaying tactic to keep from going to bed.

Karin and I were known for practicing some of those tactics, because we loved staying up at night. Of course in the morning, we had trouble getting up then, so Mama made us go to bed and then even would listen to make sure we were sleeping and not talking. But my bed was in the bedroom right by the open living room door, and Karin slept on the sofa bed right outside the door in the living room, so we could whisper to each other and Mama wouldn't hear us. We actually devised a game taking turns where we would click tunes with our tongues and the other one would guess the name of the tune. Sooner or later we would drift off to sleep of course.

Apparently on that particular night, Mama and Papa still didn't notice anything wrong when they went to bed. But sometime later Mama woke up, having to go to the bathroom, feeling really sick and woozy. She was trying to go to the window which was always open, for some fresh air, when she collapsed in the middle of the bedroom, making a terrible racket, waking all the rest of us up out of a deep sleep. If that hadn't happened, we might never have woken up at all.

It finally dawned on her that the funny smell was gas and it was strongest outside the window, so she shut the window and got us out of the bedroom and living room in a hurry. The kitchen facing out into the back yard didn't seem to be affected so that's where we spent the rest of the night. The next day it was discovered that the gas line had ruptured right below our bedroom window and the poisonous gas had drifted up into our bedroom through the open window and we definitely could have died from it.

What I find funny to this day is how Mama fretted about how awful it would have been for Karola to lose her whole family this way, not how awful it would have been for her and us to lose our lives. But that was our dear, sweet, lovable Mama! She was the eternal optimist who never gave up and who tried to find something good in everything, even in her own poor health. She suffered from chronic back pain, brought on by all the years of hard work and heavy lifting, which along with childbirth caused another condition called uterine prolapse, something bothersome and extremely unpleasant. There are easier ways to correct this now, but back then this required a major operation with a big incision in the abdomen and then the ever present danger of infection afterwards, so Mama resisted having it done for a long time.

Then Karola learned that her outfit's time at the camp was coming to an end and that they would be transferred to become telephone operators for the Army, much closer to the front. This was supposed to be done in complete secrecy and the girls were not allowed to tell anybody, but Karola told Mama anyway. Horror stories of what happened to those young, naïve and vulnerable girls abounded and were well known. Not only were they much closer to the action where they might get bombed or shot at, but they were also at the mercy of men who definitely didn't have their best interests at heart. There were even rumors that some good looking blond, blue-eyed girls ended up at breeding farms to create Hitler's "super race."

Karola, with her beautiful brown eyes and dark hair didn't have to worry about going there, at least, but Mama didn't want her going any-where. So she had her doctor attest to the fact that she needed this opera-tion and she needed her daughter home to take care of us, as she would be unable to do so. And it really worked. Karola was allowed to come home and Mama had the operation.

It was a lot of responsibility for Karola but she coped as well as she could, sending us off to school every morning, making sure we had some warm food in our tummies and a sandwich for later at recess. One thing she had trouble with was our propeller bows for our hair, so we just skipped them and didn't even miss them at all. But we did miss Mama terribly.

She was in a women's clinic, where all the nurses were Catholic nuns, which is still the case in a lot of German hospitals today. The patients were all women who had female problems or they were giving birth, which back then required at least a ten day to two week stay in the hospital in most cases. I believe Mama was in there longer than that though for her problem and we became thoroughly familiar with that hospital, we visited there so often. Our cousin Karola was in that same hospital right around that same time for surgery to correct a condition that made her unable to conceive, and we went to visit her too. She was there either a little bit before or after Mama, I don't remember which, or whom we were visiting, but I remember a lot of excitement going on there one time.

Apparently the priest had come to baptize a large group of newborn babies and the nuns were running around trying to find people to hold these babies to be sprinkled with holy water in the chapel. Some babies were so new that their mothers were still confined to their bed and not allowed to attend the baptism of their child. According to Catholic teaching, every baby was born with Eve's original sin and was doomed to purgatory if it died unless it was baptized, which made baptism so urgent and imperative.

Of course Karin and I were only too glad to help out and felt proud and honored when the nuns asked us if we would like to hold a baby for this, it's most important event. Thinking back now, I am still amazed and astounded that this happened. I was after all only nine years old at the time and Karin was ten, but we both remembered that forever.

And then, just when I thought Mama was never coming home from the hospital, leaving a great big empty spot in my heart, I came home from school one day and Karola sent me to the bedroom to get something and there was Mama sitting up in her bed smiling at me. I had never heard of "tears of joy" until then, so I was totally overwhelmed and bewildered by all the tears streaming out of my eyes at the sight of her. I was happier than I had ever been in my life and yet I was crying. I didn't understand that at all.

Mama was still weak and needed rest and had to have help with the housework, so Karola was allowed to stay home during Mama's convalescence and Mama stretched it out as long as possible to keep Karola home through the Christmas holidays. Without a doubt, Christmas has always been our most favorite holiday of the year.

Thanksgiving, which kicks off the official Christmas season here in America, is an American tradition. It's not celebrated in Germany at all, which is kind of a shame. It's not that people there aren't thankful for all the blessings in their lives every day, just nobody ever thought to turn it into a national holiday. Almost all holidays in Germany are to this day based on biblical events and connected to the church calendar.

The one exception that comes to mind is May 1st, the day for the German laborer, which may have been something Hitler came up with, I don't know for sure, but it is still being observed. Hitler, of course, had added some other holidays, namely his own birthday and other "memorable" days celebrating the "glory of the thousand year Reich," which lasted all of twelve years. People from that era still remember those days but they don't celebrate them anymore.

The official start of the Christmas season has always been the first Advent Sunday, the first of four Sundays before Christmas, when we lit that first candle on the Advent wreath. Back then, time seemed to be standing still and it felt like an eternity between Christmases, but when Mama brought that fragrant wreath home from the market and let us help with decorating it with the ribbons and four candles, we knew that the long wait would soon be over. In actuality, the season started long before that however, in early November, when everybody suddenly became very secretive, planning and working on projects and gifts to surprise other family members.

Most presents were home made back then, and the long, dreary cold and rainy November evenings when it got dark at 4:30 in the evening already, were actually quite cozy and productive. There was no television back then or any other kind of distraction and it certainly was too cold and nasty to go outside. We still had to go to school, of course in spite of the weather.

One thing we always ventured out for, no matter what, was All Saints Day, November 1st, the German Memorial Day, when everyone visited their loved ones in the cemetery. This may sound strange, but we really loved doing that, as the cemetery looked really beautiful at that time. All the graves would be decorated with fresh flowers and greenery, and with little red or white lanterns with burning candles inside, as far as the eye could see, a sight unforgettable. And the smell of those greens and the candles was equally lovely. Sometimes it would snow a little, making the tips of those greens sparkle in the candlelight, but mostly it was cold and raining, typical November weather.

December usually brought some heavy snow, along with very cold temperatures and often brilliant sunshine, perfect weather for sledding. Wurzburg, being in a valley or kettle as we call it over there, was surrounded by some pretty big hills and had some wonderful sites for sledding. A big favorite of grown-ups was the "Nikolausberg" across the river, with its long, steep incline. One could really build up some speed coming down that hill, which was also a road with traffic and therefore really too dangerous for us kids.

When Karin and I went sledding we usually headed for a little "bunny hill" in the park close to the Lions Bridge not far from where we lived. It was absolutely exhilarating to scoot down that slope and it didn't take long to walk back up it. We would do that over and over, until we finally had enough, being tired, cold and wet, but at least we didn't have far to go to get home and out of those wet clothes. Then Mama would fix us some hot tea or cocoa, all the while scolding us that we stayed out too long.

One day we always dreaded was December 6th, when every child in Germany could expect a visit from old Saint Nikolaus. This was of course the forerunner of the American Santa Clause, but contrary to the image of the jolly old guy in the red suit and the twinkle in his eye, our Nikolaus was a grumpy old man in a long dark coat with a hood, carrying a switch, actually a broom made of tied together twigs, and a list of bad things we had done.

We would be on our best behavior, nervously listening for those clunky footsteps out on the staircase and once it got dark, we usually didn't have to wait very long. He would come in the door and we would have to face him. He would ask if we had been good and of course we said "yes." Then he would pull out his list and ask, "What about this or what about that?" just amazing us with all the things he knew about us.

One time he even knew that Karin had spilled her soup that very day. We were flabbergasted! We would get a little swat on our behinds with the switch and a strong admonishment not to do those things anymore and then we would get some goodies which he fished out of the big sack he carried over his shoulder. The most memorable things we got that come to mind were a couple of adorable chocolate Santas one time that were almost too cute to eat and one time we got "Zwetschgenmannchen," little men made of prunes and nuts and other dried fruit strung on wire, which we could play with for a while and then eat.

St. Nikolaus never brought toys—that was the job of the Christkind (Christ child) on December 24, who also brought our Christmas tree at that time. Gradually over the years our doll family grew until we each had six and I especially remember the Christmas we got our celluloid dolls with the turtle mark, which was a brand new invention then. I think the year was 1942.

Karin got a girl doll and I got a boy, whom I promptly named "Peterle," everybody's favorite boy name back then. What was so remarkable about my Peterle was that he was wearing honest-to-goodness Lederhosen—pants made out of soft suede leather that Papa had made for him in the authentic Bavarian style. Everything else he wore, from the split socks and calf warmers, which Karola had knitted, to his shirt and jacket that Mama had made, was completely authentic and he even had a pair of "Haferl" shoes, a style of shoe that was only worn with Lederhosen in Bavaria. It was just about the cutest thing ever!

Karin's doll, whom she named Renate—another fashion name, even though Mama liked "Lore" better—also was dressed really cute, all made by Mama. And that pretty well became a family tradition; our main presents every year were new outfits for all our dolls. They had summer clothes and winter clothes and overcoats and hats and shoes and socks and stockings and aprons with embroidery and hand knitted sweaters. They were almost better dressed than we were ourselves!

It cost Mama countless sleepless nights to create all these lovely things and I can't even imagine all the patience it took. Officially, all these things came from the "Christkind" of course, but Mama told us that she was helping the Christkind, and she couldn't get started until we went to bed. Then we would hear her sewing machine purring until the wee hours out in the kitchen or the little room next to the kitchen. In the morning everything would be cleared away and we had no clue what she was working on except sometimes one of our dolls would be missing. Then she would say the Christkind came and got it to make new clothes for it. In reality, it was just too time consuming to redress the doll every night.

One year we got an adorable "Kleiderschrank" (clothes closet), a miniature of the one we had in our bedroom. It came with little hangers and was just the right size for all our doll clothes. And to be able to take our dolls for a walk, Karin got a really modern stroller and I got Karola's doll couch with brand new bedding in it. We also had an antique iron cradle where some of our baby dolls "slept." Our living room, which was also our playroom, really was filling up with all our toys, but nobody seemed to mind at all, because children need to play.

But life wasn't all fun and games. Mama always found plenty of chores for us to do too. One job Karin really hated was washing dishes, which she and I had to do everyday. We didn't have running hot water or soapy bubbles to make this job more pleasant. We would have to heat the water on the stove, pour it in the dishpan, add some "Imi," which was something like baking soda, to help cut the grease, but it didn't work very well. The grease always ended up on our hands, which drove Karin crazy so I always ended up washing and she did the drying.

We would have to sweep the floor and wash down all the kitchen chairs and furniture and wash the potatoes before we boiled them. Everything just seemed to be so much dirtier back then and so much harder to clean. Probably, the tight quarters we all had to share had a lot to do with that and also the wood and coal burning stove that spewed smoke and soot and ashes all over the place all the time. But nobody liked to live in filth and dirt, so everybody was always cleaning. We were also responsible to keep the staircase clean every other week, alternating with the Altenhofers across the hall.

For Christmas, we always put in a little extra elbow grease, washing curtains and all, because we wanted our place to sparkle for the holidays, and the pungent smell of paste wax and turpentine would be hanging in the air. I don't even know what Mama used that for. But eventually, all those smells would be replaced by the lovely aroma of cookies baking in the oven.

Christmas wouldn't have been the same without cookies, and in spite of strict rationing, Mama always scrounged up enough ingredients for our beloved butter cookies and "Spritzgeback" and her favorite "Springerle," which were anise flavored cookies. It was a regular family affair on the Sundays before Christmas, as everyone got into the act. Karin and I loved to sift the flour through the sifter. Mama or Karola would stir up the dough and then roll it out so we could cut it into different shapes with the little cookie cutters.

Sometimes we were allowed to roll out the dough, but Mama always cautioned us not to use too much flour or the cookies would turn into "Mehltatscherli," or flour blobs instead of butter cookies. Of course, that was just too tricky for us, because if we didn't use enough flour, the dough would get stuck on the kitchen table. We did better with the Spritz cookies which were put through the meat grinder with the cookie attachment and that definitely took two people, one to crank the handle and feed the chunks of dough in at one end, and the other to catch it at the other end and twist it into pretzels or "esses" and put it on the cookie sheet.

114

Papa was in charge of the baking. We were always hoping he would burn some, as we got to eat them right away. The rest, the good ones, would be left to cool on the wire rack and then stored in the big red cookie tin, which looked huge to us back then, with the hinged lid and old fashioned children painted on it. I believe this was one of the very few items we owned that once belonged to the grandmother I never knew, Papa's mother. We treasured it then and I still treasure it now. Back then we may have been a little more interested in the contents than the can, I have to admit though.

The whole thing would disappear for a while and Mama said the Christkind came and got it for safe keeping until Christmas, but Karin always figured out where it was hidden and sometimes we would snitch one or two. Sooner or later, Karin also always knew what we were getting for Christmas. She would find the key to the closet that Mama mysteriously kept locked this time of year and then proceed to show me what Mama was working on at night, effectively spoiling my surprise every time. But my biggest worry was that Mama would find out and get really, really angry, but she never did. Karin was always careful to put everything back exactly the way she found it. And even though it spoiled our surprise, it also enhanced our anticipation of the wonderful things that would soon be ours.

One extremely important part of Christmas was our Christstollen, which was also extremely labor-intensive to make. It was actually a two-day operation to make it. One day we would shell the almonds and then skin them by pouring boiling water over them. By the time they cooled off enough to handle, they would pop right out of that brown skin with a little coaching and squeezing. Then they had to be slivered and chopped into little pieces. The candied citrus and orange peel only came in big pieces that also had to be chopped up and the raisins and currants had to be checked and washed, as sometimes they had little stones or other impurities mixed in.

The next morning Mama would start the yeast, which would have to sit in a warm place for a while and then she would roll up her sleeves and really work up a sweat as she was kneading all that dough on the kitchen table. She would make a huge amount, enough to fill our biggest dishpan completely full and that's how we hauled it to the bakery, where the baker formed it into four or five big loaves and after letting them rise sufficiently, baked them to perfection.

But they wouldn't be complete without the coating of melted butter and powdered sugar, which had to be applied hot out of the oven. So along with the dishpan full of dough, we would also bring a bag with butter and powdered sugar and nametags for our Christstollen, to make sure somebody else wouldn't end up with them. Lots of other people also had their Christstollen baked there because German ovens were just too small to handle the large loaves, so all our Christstollen wore nametags when we brought them home.

Probably the longest day of the year for us kids was Christmas Eve, December 24. It was pretty well the same thing every year. Karin and I were banned from the living room for a few hours, while Papa was in there helping the Christkind set up the tree. Mama would keep us occupied in the kitchen with little chores while she kept flitting back and forth and sometimes disappearing for a while, then she would reappear with a progress report. "Not much longer," is what we heard a thousand times or so it seemed, but then it always was.

Mama would encourage us to sing some Christmas songs to while away the time and Karin and I would practice the poem we learned every year as a gift to Mama and Papa without their knowledge. This was actually something our teachers came up with. Every year they would have us learn a beautiful poem about Christmas. We didn't have to memorize it for school, but they suggested we do so for our parents for all the things they did for us, and Karin and I thought it was a terrific idea. She would have a different poem than I, so we would decide which one we liked better, or if they weren't too long, we would learn them both. Our all-time favorite was the one that starts, "Wald und strassen stehn verlassen," (the woods and the streets are empty now) and it goes on describing the whole Christmas atmosphere that made every Christmas so very special to us.

The presents were really only a small part of it. When the long awaited moment finally arrived, the Christkind would ring the little bell on the tree just before flying out the window, leaving it slightly ajar and that of course was our signal to step into the living room. "Silent Night" would be playing on the record player, sung by a choir that sounded like angels to us. The tree was lit with real candles and sparklers from ceiling to floor, giving the whole room a special glow and a wonderful smell. Presents weren't wrapped back then—everything was out in the open by the tree and around the room.

In the corner, Papa's manger and nativity were set up with all the wonderful figures, illuminated by hidden flashlight bulbs and batteries to remind us of the reason for the season. The table would be set with Mama's best china, the set with the gold rim, for our Christmas eve supper, which usually was potato salad and ham or pork chops because that could be cooked ahead and then put on hold until after the gift giving. When "Silent Night" was over, Karin and I would recite our poem to Mama and Papa and then we would dive into our presents, with all the "oohs" and "ahs" that delighted Mama and Papa.

German children didn't get stockings with goodies in them. That is not a German custom. We got Christmas plates filled with goodies, such as chocolate, fruit, nuts, and the cookies we had baked and maybe gingerbread. I don't remember any kind of toys in the plates. To us a special treat were the oranges that were getting rarer and rarer as the war dragged on, but somehow the government always came through with a ration of oranges from Italy.

After supper, we always got to stay up late to play with our new toys and munch on cookies and Christstollen while Papa played Christmas music. When it was finally time to go to bed, I almost envied Karin a little bit because she got to sleep in the Christmas room with all its coziness and wonderful aroma that lingers in my memory to this very day. Trees were fresh cut back then and incredibly fragrant. They were so green and moist that one didn't have to worry about them catching on fire with the burning candles on them.

Papa always waited to the last moment any way to buy a tree, because we had no place to store it. I remember one year he put it out on the roof, tying it to the windowsill and he may have done that other years too. Of course since he waited so late the choices weren't so great and Mama always complained about it, when he first brought it home. But he always managed to turn it into a masterpiece.

He would get some extra branches to fill in the gaps by drilling little holes into the trunk and gluing in the branches. Of course, we didn't know that back then, I just know that we always had a beautiful tree, with all the shining glass ornaments, some of them dusted with sparkling "snow," and little glass birds and bells and glass icicles that looked like the real thing hanging off our eaves. All the candles were in silver candleholders that clipped to the branches and then there were fine strands of tinsel—not too much, just a little. According to Papa, less was more in this case.

Like so many other holidays in Germany, Christmas was a two-day affair. The first day we stayed home, playing with our new toys or games, while Mama cooked her Hasenpfeffer, or rabbit stew, which tasted delicious to us, and there would be music and a general feeling of love, peace and harmony, even in the middle of this terrible war. The second day, we would visit our Tante Marie and her gang and exchange gifts with them and spend another fun-filled day.

School never started back up until after January 6, another German holiday—the day of the three kings who came to visit baby Jesus in Bethlehem. And the tree definitely wasn't taken down before that. It was not unusual to still see Christmas trees at the end of January and some people left theirs up until Easter. In our cramped little space, that would have been impossible, so usually sometime in the middle of January, the tree had to go, no matter how much we loved it, and we made a family ritual out of it too.

Papa would take down the ornaments, handing them to us kids and we would carefully dust and polish them and put them in their original boxes for safe storage. Even the tinsel was carefully removed, straightened and wrapped up for next time—not a strand was left on the tree. Then the tree was cut up and piece by piece burned in the kitchen and living room stoves, smelling wonderful even then, and making the whole place really warm.

But before all that happened, there was another very important day to celebrate—actually two—one of them being Karin's birthday, December 30th, but it kind of got lost quite often since it was right after Christmas (poor Karin). The day we really looked forward to was New Year's Eve.

As far back as I can remember, Mama always let us stay up to toast the New Year with a sip of the hot wine punch that was so much a part of New Year's Eve. The whole family would gather at Tante Marie's house, sloshing through some of the worst weather imaginable or sometimes deep snow just to be together to celebrate the New Year. The evening would begin with a nice meal, and then we would play all kinds of funny party games and tell jokes and stories until it was time to make the punch, which was a big deal of course.

It required red wine and white wine and some hot tea and rum and fresh-squeezed oranges and sugar and cinnamon sticks, all heated to just below the boiling point and of course it had to be ready just before midnight. Sometimes it was a mad scramble just to get all the punch cups filled by the last stroke of the clock. Such a special brew of course had to be served out of a very special container, and I still remember how proud Mama was when she was able to buy our crockery punchbowl with images of German castles on it—truly a work of art, just beautiful!

We hauled it to Tante Marie's house along with extra food and wine and cookies and other things for the party. Unfortunately, the first time she ever poured the hot punch into the cold punch bowl; it got a crack in the bottom and just about broke Mama's heart. But we used it for many years thereafter, we just set it on a plate because it leaks a little—and I still own it to this day. It also survived the war obviously. Back then, a year seemed like a very long time to us.

Eleven

Maybe what made New Year's Eve so exciting to us was just to get rid of the old and bring in the new. Everyone was filled with hope and anticipation of what this new year would bring, as we clinked our glasses together and shouted "Prost Neujahr," with great enthusiasm. But in spite of all our best hopes, things would only get worse every year, for a very long time.

Nobody had to worry about their waistline any more as our rations got smaller from month to month. Our city was crowded with people fleeing the big industrial cities that were being bombed to smithereens. All the hospitals were filled to capacity with wounded soldiers from the front. In spite of all the glowing reports of victory in the newspapers, we knew that the war in Russia was going very badly for us. Thousands of men were killed, captured or were missing and were never heard from again.

Very few families were left untouched by this great tragedy and we went to quite a lot of funerals during this time. So far, the funerals were for people that we weren't really that close to, such as Frau Altenhofer's brother or a cousin of Mama's whom I didn't really know personally. But we loved his mother, Mama's favorite aunt. She was a very sweet lady who was completely devastated. She only had two sons and the other one was also in Russia.

We were painfully aware of all the heartbreak and uncertainty this war was causing, as people were living for the mail every day, hoping for letters from their loved ones that seldom or never came. How lucky we were to have Papa home safe and sound! But now we had to worry about Karola again.

Mama had gotten better, so Karola had to finish her obligation with the Arbeitsdienst. This time she was assigned to a bomb factory in Furth near Nurnberg, of which there were several in the area. It was a very dangerous job, making bombs and detonators, and we were always looking for mail from her that would tell us that she was all right. One time we thought for sure that we had lost her, when several of the factories were bombed, causing tremendous explosions of the material inside, but miraculously she escaped and I believe she even sent a telegram that time to let us know.

It was a huge relief when she was finally finished with the Arbeitsdienst and was able to come home to stay. Through Papa's connections, she got a job selling tickets at the railroad station in Zell, just outside Wurzburg. It was a job she really liked and much safer than making bombs, but not long after she started working there, the station was bombed and she again just barely escaped with her life. It was a random bombing with hardly any warning at all. The only shelter available to her there was the underpass that led to the railroad track and everybody made a mad dash for that.

But then the buildings near the entrance started collapsing, closing it off and burying some people underneath the rubble. Karola, who was further back in the underpass, could hear them screaming under the rubble, until there was an eerie silence. I don't know how many people lost their lives there. The rest, including Karola, were trapped in total darkness in the underpass and had to dig their own way out from inside with their bare hands.

A few other areas were hit at the same time, some not all that far from us across the river, resulting in quite a few deaths, because of the surprise attack. I have to admit, we did go over there to gawk, and couldn't believe the destruction a few bombs could cause. But nobody wanted to believe that our beloved Wurzburg was a target.

We had after all, no kind of war industry whatsoever and all the big buildings had been converted into hospitals for the wounded and had huge red crosses painted on the roofs. Wurzburg was a treasure from way back, known for its many beautiful churches and its big university, where Winston Churchill, our arch enemy, had studied as a young man. Surely he wouldn't bomb our beautiful town!

People were so complacent; they actually loved standing in the street watching formations of planes flying over high up in the sky like huge flocks of silver birds, headed for points east. Only weeks earlier we ourselves had been standing on the Altenhofer's flat roof, basking in the sunshine and watching wave after wave of planes flying toward Schweinfurt and dropping incredible amounts of bombs on that small town where our uncle lived, about thirty miles away.

The aftermath of fire and smoke billowing hundreds of meters into the sky could be clearly seen and was totally awe-inspiring. But Schweinfurt had lots of industry and was known worldwide for its precision quality ball bearings—indispensable in keeping all sorts of things moving smoothly. Small wonder that the enemy wanted to wipe that off the face of the earth.

There now was a big banner on the front of our train station with the ominous message, "Rader mussen rollen fur den krieg—kopfe mussen rollen fur den sieg." (Wheels must roll for the war—heads must roll for victory!) Nazis were very big on banners with messages. They were strung up all over town. What was missing were all of our beautiful statues made of metal.

Even the four big lions on the Lion's Bridge had disappeared along with all the church bells. Supposedly they had been stored away for safekeeping, but everybody suspected that they would be melted down to make bullets. We just figured we would never see them again, but some of them actually did survive the war, including the lions.

All in all, and in spite of everything, life went on and people had to go to work even if their stomachs were growling, and children had to go to school. Things such as gym and swimming were suspended as it involved large groups of children walking to another school that had a gym and walking to the "hallenbad," the big indoor swimming pool in Wurzburg. It was eventually closed for lack of coal for heating. Classes were often interrupted by bomb alerts when everyone had to go to the basement under the school, but like everything else in Peterschule, it was totally inadequate and wouldn't have offered much protection. The building had a raised first floor, so the basement was only half underground.

Swimming was taught in the fourth grade, once a week, but by the time I got there it had been suspended. Karin actually had a few lessons, but then she was offered an opportunity to Schillerschule, because of overcrowding and she jumped at the chance. Her teacher, Fraulein Seufert was known as "the battle axe of Peterschule," and no one escaped her wrath, even Karin who was normally well-liked by all her teachers. Her "crime" was that she stood up for one of her best friends, Rosemarie Pfaff, a beautiful blond girl with porcelain skin and ruby red rosebud lips.

Frl. Seufert accused Rosemarie that she was wearing lipstick, which wasn't true and Karin told the teacher so. She knew her lips were always red like that. For that, both of them got hit three times on the palms with the Spanish rod, Frl. Seufert's favorite method of discipline. My turn came a year later when I also had Frl. Seufert in fourth grade and I was punished exactly the same way for coming back from a bathroom break a little bit after the class had already returned. It hurt so bad, it took all the strength I could muster to keep from crying. For all the mental cruelty Frl. Ewald had inflicted on me the previous three years, at least she never hit me like that and I almost wished I had her back.

Karin loved her new teacher and had no trouble making friends at the new school. It was twice as far to walk as Peterschule, but it was well worth it to her. Her new friends included girls whose fathers were doctors or dentists, coming from a whole different world than the kids from the Kaserne we sat next to in Peterschule, and the teachers actually communicated with parents.

Karin was fast approaching a cross road by the end of the fourth grade. She could continue in public school until eighth grade and then get out and learn a trade, or she could go to private "oberschule" starting with fifth grade to pursue a higher education all the way through college, which had always been limited to the well-to-do because of the high cost of tuition and books. Being a straight-A student, she definitely qualified for higher education and her teacher recognized that, but apparently also recognized that this was out of the reach of people of our income level. Luckily, even back then, people knew that "a mind was a terrible thing to waste," and in spite of all the evil Hitler did, he believed strongly in education and he created an "oberschule" for gifted children that was completely free, with the exact same curriculum, such as advanced math, science, foreign languages and art.

This is what the teacher recommended for Karin and Mama and Papa saw this as a terrific opportunity for Karin and it turned out to be just that. Instead of drudgery, school was now stimulating and interesting and no one had to wait for slow readers anymore. There were none as everyone knew how to read. The teachers were kind and helpful, not mean and nasty. It sounded wonderful to me.

My biggest hope was that I was gifted enough to qualify for "Hauptschule" too, as it was called. I knew I could never measure up to Karin's brilliance—she excelled at every subject—but my report card was actually very good, it just wasn't straight-A's. I had a few B's in there too, usually. Of course, first I had to make it through Frl. Seufert's fourth grade, quite a challenge, and at the same time I had taken on another challenge.

Mama had always absolutely loved accordion music, so much so that Papa said he could probably learn to play it for her if only he had an accordion. So Mama secretly saved up slowly, mark by mark, enough money to surprise him with one. It cost one hundred marks, a small fortune back then. My best guess is that this was around 1941 or 1942. What a surprise for Papa!

He made a valiant effort at learning it, took lessons as his shift work allowed and practiced whenever he had time, which was very little. Papa worked so much, he didn't have any spare time, and there were always more pressing needs. So he stopped the lessons and then he stopped playing and the accordion sat in the corner in the living room. Every so often Mama would look at it and say with a big sigh that she had three girls, but none of them wanted to learn to play this beautiful accordion for her, laying on the guilt really thick.

Maybe it was the guilt or maybe I wanted to earn some extra "Brownie points" with Mama or maybe it was the fact that it meant so much to her that I said I would learn it for her. It seemed like such a small thing to do, when she had done so much for me already—nursing me through countless very serious illnesses, sitting up with me and watching over me when she was dead tired herself and not in the best of health either. Mama was thrilled that I wanted to do this and then her practical side took over.

First of all, I had to prove that I could carry the accordion, which was pretty big and heavy for a little squirt like me (I could, by the way). Then we had to find a teacher that was within walking distance and that didn't cost an arm and a leg. Frau Karl on Buttnergasse met all those requirements, but the only problem was that she had no openings.

By then Bubi Sauer, our friend's red-haired son from the Kaserne had been studying with Frau Karl for three years already and she told his mother frankly that she had taught Bubi all she knew and there was nothing else she could teach him. So Bubi stopped going and I got his spot. Bubi was a wonderful player and he had a beautiful accordion his brother-in-law had brought back from Italy, where probably the world's best accordions were made. He would come over every so often and play for us, just dazzling us with his ability and making it all look so easy, playing all our favorite songs for us.

I could only hope to ever be even half as good as he was, but when Frau Karl wanted me to play the keys with my right hand and push the buttons with my left, I knew that I had bitten off more than I could chew. My fingers just simply did not want to do that. There was no way. It was impossible, and I thought it couldn't be done. But Frau Karl was a patient soul and kept encouraging me to practice, practice, practice!

That was the real secret to success and eventually, I got the hang of it. My left hand could actually do something entirely different than my right one, all at the same time. That's not to say that I was good or pleasant to listen to. Frau Karl believed very much in communicating with the parents to keep them informed about their child's progress and she was forever writing notes to take home. One note sticks in my mind to this very day.

It said, "Please encourage your child to play softer, as she is playing unbearably loud," with those last two words underlined several times. By then I was already playing simple little folk songs and Mama was so thrilled that she didn't even notice that I was playing "unbearably loud," apparently and neither did I. An accordion's loudness is determined by the force with which the bellows is pulled and pushed with the left hand, so I simply had to learn not to yank or push so hard on the bellows.

Frau Karl was a very thorough teacher, and besides playing softer, I also had to not only learn to read music, but also learn to write it with perfectly shaped notes, clefs, and piano keys. Anything less than perfect was unacceptable. She was tough, but she was kind and she got results. By Christmas, just a few weeks into my training, I was able to play some Christmas songs for Mama on Christmas Eve. That made her very happy.

After a while, Frau Karl also added singing to my training. She would play the piano and I had to sing "mu-nu-lu" up and down the scale (not do-re-mi). I am still mystified as to what that was all about. Obviously I didn't get much out of that because I still can't sing well. Sometimes I wonder if Bubi also had to sing mu-nu-lu. I never asked him though, and he couldn't sing either.

Between Frau Karl's and Frl. Seufert's never ending demands and all the chores at home that still had to be done, it was a busy year, as it was for Karin with all the new things she had to learn. To me, one of the most exciting subjects she was learning was English. I desperately wanted to learn that too. To be able to communicate in another language seemed like an almost unattainable dream back then to us.

Much later we realized that learning English fit right in with Hitler's plan to rule the world. Of course we needed to speak the language if we were going to conquer England and America. It may sound laughable and ridiculous now, but that's exactly what Hitler had in mind and he was deadly serious about it. With constant and relentless propaganda, he tried to brainwash us kids and turn us into little Nazis.

At age ten, we had to join the Hitler Youth, whether we wanted to or not, with mandatory weekly meetings where we were indoctrinated. On Saturday mornings we had to learn marching together, wearing our uniforms—white shirts and navy skirts. Once we got the hang of it, we felt quite important marching through town in lock-step singing at the top of our lungs, "Group Eleven coming here, Group Eleven coming here, tra-ra, tra-ra," and other songs. People would just stop and look and shake their heads. One of the girls up front would be carrying a pennant on a long stick with the number eleven on it. It was all heady stuff for little girls and hard not to get caught up in it.

One of the first official functions group eleven (my group) participated in was a huge rally which started at the Residenzplatz, the big cobblestone square in front of the Residenz. All different branches of the military were there, with lots of swastika flags, and there were bands playing and all age groups of Hitler youth, boys and girls, and there were loud speakers for all the speeches to be heard loud and clear. This lasted most of the afternoon, then everyone marched through town, across the river and up the hill to the "Festung," the famous castle up on the hill. By then, it had gotten dark so there were tall torches stuck into the ground at intervals to light the way and illuminate the walls of the castle. It was so incredibly beautiful that it is hard to describe. There were more speeches at the castle and more music and then we went back to the Residenzplatz.

The evening culminated in all the fourteen year old boys being loaded in big trucks to go off to the war. I can still see all the mothers standing there crying and clinging to their sons in one last embrace and the boys trying to be very brave, but looking very scared and lost. So this is what this whole thing was about—a big send-off for children to fight a totally hopeless war! The ceremony was stirring and spectacular—the Nazis were masters at that sort of thing—but the purpose behind it was absolutely sinister and horrifying.

All along, Papa had pointed out to us the futility of this war. Every time we were flipping through the atlas to plan a trip, Papa would turn to the world map to show us the big picture of what we were up against. Here was Russia on the right as big as his whole hand he would say, and there was America on the left, as big as his other hand, and in the middle there was Germany, as big as his thumbnail, fighting them both. How ridiculous! Even little girls like us could see what a hopeless and impossible situation we were in.

Anyone who said anything to that effect was considered to be an enemy of the state, with dire consequences. We were constantly reminded of the "duties" we had toward our "Fatherland," and the sacrifices we were expected to make for it. There were no more trips after Salzburg. With massive troop movements and people fleeing the big cities and other dangerous areas, the trains were now horribly over-crowded and very unsafe, because they were also being bombed quite often. Munich had been bombed several times and there really was no safe place to visit anymore—anywhere.

But, like all children, we were looking forward to our summer vacation anyway. It only lasts six weeks in Germany as school goes all the way through the middle of July, and then starts back up again at the end of August, or early September. To us it meant six glorious weeks of freedom. What we particularly looked forward to every summer was the fair called "Killianifest," which just happened to start right around the beginning of our school vacation, and it just happened to set up along the Main River, not very far from where we lived.

There were all sorts of fun rides—very tame by today's standards—and there were puppet shows and flea circus and dancing dogs and even a two-headed woman, which was very obviously fake, and there were ice cream stands and hot dog stands and games of chance, of course, just wonderful stuff and very cheap. Money was always tight at our house, but Mama would give us a few pfennigs anyway and we would go off and have a blast.

One year we got it into our heads to raise some extra money for the fair by putting on a play for all the neighborhood children. Our collaborators in this endeavor were Rosemarie Pfaff, whose red lips had gotten Karin into big trouble with her teacher, and Rosemarie's twin sister Anneliese, two girls who lived just two houses down from us above the guesthouse, and with whom we were quite inseparable back then.

The only material we had were our fairy tale books, so we picked a story that had especially touched us named "Snow White and Rose Red," and turned it into a play. I can't remember the story too well anymore, but somehow it was determined that us two Rosemaries had to play the lead roles, the blond one was Snow White, and I with my darker hair and complexion was Rose Red. Karin played our brother who had been turned into a bear by some nasty ogre; at least I think that's how the story went.

I don't know if there was a part for Anneliese too, but I know she was terrific at selling tickets and promoting our show all over the neighborhood, and then herding every one into our little backyard, which had a natural stage built in. Actually it was a raised area on one side with a clothesline from which we hung blankets, which served as our curtain. We had a good turnout and I guess everybody liked it, at least nobody asked for their money back. To us, the money we earned meant an extra ride or two on the merry-go-round, or on the "yo-yo" that was our favorite.

Like so many other things in Germany, this festival was steeped in ancient history, dating all the way back to the year 686, when Bishop Killian of Irish-Scottish descent brought Christianity to Wurzburg and baptized its leader, Earl Gosbert. Only three years later in 689, Gosbert's daughter-in-law Gailana had Killian and his helpers Kolonat and Totnan beheaded because Killian had declared her marriage to Gosbert's son Hedan illegal and invalid. Besides the fair, the festival always included a reenactment of this dastardly deed, with mock beheadings of course.

I'm not sure what happened to Gailana, but apparently she couldn't stop the spread of Christianity even in her own family. Hedan, her illegal husband later built a church in the castle square up on the hill, parts of which can still be seen and are believed to be the oldest stone building east of the Rhine River in Germany. He dedicated it to the Virgin Mary and to this day the castle and the hill it sits on are named Marienburg and Marienberg after Mary. Killian, Kolonat and Totnan became martyrs whose bones were disinterred and preserved and became relics that are revered to this day. Killian was later declared a saint and Wurzburg became known as "the city of Killian." There are statues of all three martyrs on the Old Saints Bridge that leads from the city across the river up to the castle.

We were attracted to the river even when there was no fair. Sometimes we would all take our doll buggies out to the meadows along the river's edge for a picnic and let our dolls go wading in the shallow water. One time Karin's brand new doll Renate almost floated away from her. I don't think Karin would have deliberately drowned herself if that had happened, but it sure would have been hard to explain to Mama, and Karin would have been in big trouble. Back then we didn't even know that the same fate had almost befallen Karin herself, when Karola was supposed to watch her years earlier.

Not too far past where we went picnicking, there was a ferry that hauled people across the river. It was just a very simple boat with benches running the length of the boat on each side, powered by a man with a long pole standing in the rear. Meter by meter he would push this boat full of people across the river. It was fascinating to watch and the most peaceful feeling, to let our hands trail in the water and bask in the sunshine. We loved riding this ferry and actually felt very safe in it. No one wore life vests, there were none, but we had never heard of anything bad ever happening to anyone. Apparently, the river was fairly shallow at that point, but it was definitely deep enough to drown in.

On the other side, a section of the river had been turned into a beautiful swimming area with lifeguards and slides and diving boards and pools of all different depths. We went there sometimes as a family, but Mama wouldn't let us go there alone. It was just too big and the potential of something happening to us was very real to her. So sometimes we would just ride the ferry for no apparent reason, hang out on the other side for a little while and then ride back.

There was another place for swimming, also across the river, but much closer to home that Mama didn't mind us going to. This was actually a big boat anchored halfway between the Lions Bridge and the Old Saints Bridge that was set up like a swimming pool with wooden bottoms and open sides for the water to enter. It had cabins where one could change clothes. It also had a ferry, but I believe it was motorized. We really loved going there in the summer, because it was such a fun place with two pools, a deep one for swimming (we stayed out of that one) and a shallow one for frolicking that was just right for us.

This was actually the first swimming pool for ladies only that was created somewhere around the latter part of the nineteenth century. The cabins were surrounding the pools on all sides, to shield bathers from the prying eyes of men, even though bathing costumes covered every inch of the female body back then. People were very modest back then! Of course, by the time we were using the pool, all that had changed and it was open to both sexes wearing "normal" bathing suits, not two-piece or bikinis. Those came much later and were quite shocking at first. How times have changed!

Little did we know that we were experiencing the end of an era when the pool closed in the fall of 1943 as it did every fall because it would never open again. Everything else that made our summer so much fun ended that year. There were no more trips, no fair, no ferry rides, and no pool. Everything was strictly about survival now, as things got tougher all the way around. Food and other daily needs, already severely rationed, were in such short supply that there were long lines for everything.

Bakeries especially were hard pressed to keep pace with the demand as they were now ordered to also supply nearby cities such as Schweinfurt, Nurnberg and Aschaffenburg that had all been severely bombed already and had no possibility of taking care of their own needs. But along with limited supplies such as flour, there was also a shortage of power for the ovens. Bakers would only be allotted a few hours on different days of work. Needless to say, when word got out that a bakery was baking, it would spread like wildfire and everyone would rush there to stand in line for a few hours for a loaf of bread, only to go home empty handed quite often because there just wasn't enough for everybody.

To make matters worse, it seemed that our potato crop, the mainstay of the German diet, was now also under attack. The "enemy" of the potato is a nasty little brown and yellow beetle that feasts on the greenery above the ground, preventing the potatoes in the ground from growing properly. An extraordinarily heavy infestation of these beetles had been found in many areas, along with open pouches of unknown origin, probably thrown out of enemy airplanes. So now, once school ended in July, it was our duty as Hitler youths to walk the fields from morning until evening looking for potato beetles.

We would march to the fields at the edge of town, singing and pumped with propaganda and enthusiasm. Some very cranky old teachers, Frl. Seufert among them, who were very unhappy to be there, met us at the fields to supervise us. We were shown pictures of what we were looking for and even promised a reward for every beetle we found. It was hot and dusty walking every row of these fields all day long. There was no shade anywhere and absolutely nothing to drink at all and our enthusiasm waned pretty quickly.

By the time we were allowed to head home, we were a pretty bedraggled, exhausted bunch that didn't care if we marched in lockstep or not. We were sunburned and our shoes were ruined and nobody had found one beetle. Mama was so angry she didn't want us to go anymore and she ignored the postcard they sent that informed us of our next date with the potato fields. Then Papa got a very threatening letter inquiring why he had failed to do his duty of making us do ours. He had to come up with all kinds of excuses in writing that prevented us from doing our duty and promise that this would never happen again, but we were still worried about repercussions. Such is life in a totalitarian system!

Eventually the potatoes were harvested and in spite of everything, there were a lot less of them and they were also rationed now. Everyone was constantly reminded to boil them in the jacket to avoid waste. Peeling potatoes raw resulted in a thicker peel to be thrown away and there were actually people who checked other people's garbage cans to see who didn't boil their potatoes before peeling and therefore were an "enemy of the state." Our butter and sugar ration was now so miniscule, it was almost non-existent and we were so hungry for something sweet to put on our bread in the morning (when we even had bread!).

One time on our way home from Tante Marie's house, we succumbed to temptation and dug up a big bag full of sugar beets from a field we had to pass. This of course was stealing and we were scared to death of being caught while doing it. Mama cut them up and boiled them until they turned into a brown, gooey syrup. It takes a lot of beets to make a little syrup though and was hardly worth the effort and the guilt. I believe those beets were mainly grown to be fed to livestock in the winter, not to make sugar. The animals had to eat too, after all, to keep producing milk.

Twelve

I don't know if it was due to lack of proper nutrition or maybe just not enough of it, that my health took another very serious nosedive in the spring of 1944. After the long, cold and dreary winters everyone always longs for spring in Germany and this was one of those days, when the air was milder and the sun was stronger and the birds were singing. As Karin was leaving for school, I was wishing with all of my heart that I could go too, but I was stuck in bed with tonsillitis again. But it hardly hurt anymore and my fever was down. It would just be a few more days of recuperation and I would be fine again.

Then my nose started bleeding, just a trickle at first. Mama told me to just lie still, flat on my back and maybe it would stop. She had to leave for a while, and I don't know where she had to go, but when she got back my nose was still bleeding and the flow was getting stronger and eventually started gushing. Mama put cold, wet rags on my head and face, but that didn't help. The blood was running down my throat and burning my tonsils, and I could hardly swallow fast enough, I felt like I was drowning in my own blood and nothing would stop it.

For the first time in my life, I saw Mama looking really scared and helpless and when I asked her if I was going to die, she shook her head, but she started to cry. I knew for sure that I was going to die then, but I couldn't even cry because it made my nose bleed more and I was so busy swallowing. About three hours into this ordeal, Dr. Mertz came and suggested that we get some ice from the guesthouse. By then Karin had come home from school and she ran and got a big bowl full of ice which they packed all over my head and neck, and incredibly, it stemmed the flood and the bleeding stopped.

What a relief for everybody, especially me! I was still alive, but just barely, feeling really weak and sick. My bed was soaking wet from all the wet rags and melted ice, so Mama helped get me out if it and had me sit in a chair while she was getting fresh linens and then I got sick on my stomach. All the blood I had swallowed had clotted and was now coming out, proceeding to fill a foot tub that we used to wash our feet in. There was so much of it that it was hard to believe that I had any left in my body at all. It was pretty disgusting even for me and it had to be horrifying for anyone who saw it, I imagine.

I felt so bad for having put Mama through all that, and now I also had a terrible fear of nosebleeds, which took almost a lifetime to overcome. But, aside from little normal nosebleeds, nothing like that ever happened to me again, thank goodness. I'm not at all sure if there was a connection, but besides this problem, I also had a sleep disorder and maybe that's not even the right word for it. I just could not wake up, once I was in a deep sleep at night.

This was very bad, because now we had bomb alerts on a regular basis in the middle of the night. Large squadrons of enemy planes would be observed heading straight for Wurzburg, so the sirens would be blaring to get everybody up and into the bomb shelters. Usually the planes would make a sharp turn to the east or south or both, by splitting up, just before reaching our city, but of course no one could be sure of that. Every alert could have been the real thing, therefore it was an absolute "no no" to go to the shelter in pajamas. We would have to get fully dressed, shoes and all, just in case.

My problem was that I couldn't wake up and never heard the siren or anything. Karin had the opposite problem. She was a nervous wreck and couldn't sleep at all anymore. She later told me about how Mama would haul me into the kitchen and tell me to get dressed and I would be sound asleep, never hearing a word she said. So Mama would have to get us both dressed and get us into the basement as quickly as possible. In a way we were lucky that our basement was deemed suitable as a bomb shelter. Not everybody had that "luxury" and had to go to public shelters.

It was now against the law not to go to a shelter when there was an alert. Of course, since it was mandatory to go to a shelter, everybody had to be assigned to one. This had to be quite an undertaking to provide reasonably safe shelters for that many people. At that time there were about 100,000 people living in Wurzburg, plus an estimated 100,000 wounded soldiers in the hospitals and there had to be room for people traveling through and visitors.

The first choice was always people's basements, but not everyone had one or they were just not safe enough and even the ones that were had to have modifications to offer maximum protection. Every shelter had to have at least one emergency exit other than the stairs in case the house collapsed and blocked the staircase. In a lot of cases this was achieved by creating "breakthroughs" to the neighboring basements on both sides. Whole long rows of houses were connected that way, where one could just climb through these breakthroughs from one basement to the next in hopes of finding an escape route. This actually proved to be a very good idea that saved countless lives when the bombing actually started.

In the meantime, the breakthroughs were lightly bricked over with material that was easily removable to prevent mischief and give people some measure of control and privacy. When our basement was checked out, it was determined right away that there was no possibility for a breakthrough because the tiny Bitter's house next door had no basement. Our house was at the end of the line, more or less. For some reason, I can't remember a breakthrough to the house on the other side either. I don't think there was one, but I could be wrong.

Our basement consisted of two sections, one larger one at the foot of the slightly curving stone stairs and a narrower one next to it, which was divided into cubicles where everyone stored their potatoes and coal. A solid stone wall separated the two sections, with a doorway close to the bottom of the stairs leading to the cubicles. The ceiling appeared to have been hewn out of solid rock, with curved areas typical of the passage ways of ancient churches and cloisters, and it was believed that there had been such a passageway at one time from the Reurer Kirche (the church up the street) to the Main River and even under the river up to the castle. Speculation was that it had also been much deeper at one time but it had been partially filled in with dirt and our hard packed dirt floor could have been evidence of that. It was a very solid structure, like a fortress almost, and perfect for a bomb shelter.

The only problem was that it was prone to flooding. At the spring thaw after a particularly bitter winter when the Main River was at its flood stage, we could expect water in the basement. It only happened once or twice in my memory but it was an eerie feeling to have the Main sloshing around underneath us. In spite of all that, all the modifications were made to turn our basement into a proper bomb shelter.

First of all, a wall was built with a very heavy door, similar to a freezer locker door, to turn the area at the foot of the stairs into a "safe room." To be able to escape from there in case the door was blocked, a breakthrough was created to be able to climb into the cubicle area—actually another little room at the end of the cubicles. This place had a narrow little window close to the ceiling at street level for ventilation. This was enlarged somewhat, enough so people could fit through it (remember, no one was very big back then!). Iron rungs were put into the wall to get up to the window.

To protect the window at street level, a concrete shelter was built, much like a lean-to with openings on each side for crawling out. The break-through also was covered with a very heavy door with a freezer locker-type closure. It was very well thought out, and it gave us some sense of security and hope for survival. At the same time, we were still hoping that it would never have to stand the test of the times.

One thing we really liked was the electric light that was strung down the stairs and into the safe room. That meant no more fumbling with candles or flashlights with weak batteries, but everyone still kept those things close at hand, as the power supply was sporadic and not at all reli-able. Every house had to have an air raid warden whose main function was to make sure everyone who was assigned to the shelter was present and accounted for during an air raid—just in case they didn't hear the siren.

Mama, who absolutely didn't want the job, was appointed and was forced to accept it. She even got a gas mask along with instructions on how to use it, in case she had to search smoke and gas filled (from broken gas lines) rooms for people who were supposed to be in the shelter. We had a really good laugh the first time she tried it on, it looked so funny on her. And then of course, we all had to try it on, but aside from being too big for us, it was very confining and unpleasant, and smelled bad too, like rubber.

At the same time the basement was prepared, the attic was also in-spected for fire hazards and other dangerous conditions, of which quite a few were found. Since the apartments were so small, everybody had lots of excess things stored up there, all behind lockable wooden partitions, because people really didn't trust each other. All that had to be cleared out now and the partitions had to be torn down, leaving one big open space under the slanted roof.

The safe room was also one big open space, so we were allowed to put some kind of seating for each person down there along with some survival gear, within reason of course, due to the limited space. I don't know if we were distracted with me being sick or exactly what happened, but next thing you know there were two iron bedsteads with mattresses down there along the walls on each side of the entrance door, leaving a walkway between the two beds, which was now half blocked by a table of fairly good size.

One of the beds and the table belonged to the Altenhofers who needed a lot of seating for all their kids, so they put a bed down there, where they could sit and also take turns stretching out a little bit. Their family wasn't quite as large as it used to be though, as Herr Altenhofer had also been drafted and was serving in the German Navy and Lulu was serving first in the Arbeitsdienst and after that in the infantry. Elsee had gone to live with her aunt permanently and Anni was only there about half the time, often staying with her other grandmother, Frau Dehler and one of her aunts, who lived with Frau Dehler. This left Frau Altenhofer and the three younger boys Max, Karl (who was known as Karlmann) and George, and their other grandmother, the "old" Frau Altenhofer, who was our landlady, but she preferred to sit on a chair.

The other bed belonged to the Alberts who lived two floors below us on the bottom floor. These people were the "outcasts" of Landwehrstrasse 9, and everyone was in a state of war with them the whole time we lived there. They were suspected of being communists, which was the same as saying "scum of the earth," even worse than being a "Nazi." There was an older man, Herr Albert and his very thin, sickly wife who had severe asthma and could only speak in whispers, and their daughter, Gretel, a very loud, brash woman and her son Erich, who as the same age as I. Erich apparently took after his grandmother, as he was very sickly and he was so white, he may have been an albino, but we didn't know about those things back then. Unlike his mother, he never went outside and we rarely saw him. But Gretel and her mother loved hanging out of the window right by the front door watching all the comings and goings and making snide remarks to us kids.

Sometimes they would yell at us for being too loud when we were playing outside, or for letting the door slam, or for coming down the wooden stairs like a "thundering herd of buffalos."

This quite often resulted in a terrible shouting match with Frau Altenhofer and Mama shouting from above to leave us kids alone, and Gretel shouting back, and of course it always escalated into a whole list of other grievances—a very unpleasant situation. Unfortunately we had to go right by their door to get in or out of the house and sometimes we were afraid that they might attack us, but they never did. Sometimes Gretel actually made us laugh, when we heard her singing very loud and very off-key inside the apartment with the windows wide open. Anyway, those were the people who occupied the other bed in the basement.

There were still more people besides us five who had to share this same small space. There was a very old couple, the Rohrbachers, who lived on the second floor. They just put two chairs at the foot of the Altenhofer's bed for them to sit on. And then there were the Bitters from next door, who staked out the small area next to the Rohrbachers. They also consisted of five people—Frau Bitter, her three children Hansi, Annie, and Heini, ages 13, 12 and 11, and Frau Bitter's father Herr Seemann. They were a very nice family who had already seen more than their share of tragedy.

Frau Bitter was expecting her fourth baby just a couple of years earlier, when her husband was found hanging in his workshop one morning. No one knows what might have led this man to do such a thing and at the same time put such a stigma on his family. Frau Bitter was still deep in mourning when she gave birth to little Michael who was actually the first baby on the block in a long time. Annie would push him up and down the street in his baby carriage and everyone would flock around to look at him, he was so cute and everyone just loved him.

Frau Bitter's father came to live with them and he was a very quiet, friendly man and things seemed to be getting better for the family. Then, when Michael was about ten months old, he got diphtheria and died in the hospital very suddenly. It was so sad and the whole neighborhood mourned little Michael. Since they had no basement of their own, they were assigned to our shelter. I can't recall what kind of seating they had, but I know there wasn't room for any more beds for anyone else.

Mama was actually kind of resentful about that. All we had was a corner at the foot of Albert's bed, but we couldn't use it to it's fullest because this is where the breakthrough was and it had to be left accessible. As it happens, we had some big wooden crates up in the attic, which had to be removed and one of them fit perfectly into that corner. Mama proceeded to fill it full of all her good china, glass wear, punch bowl, and other treasures and then covered it with the mattress from the crib I used to sleep in, so we would have a soft place to sit during the long hours we sat in the basement. This was actually almost better than a bed because it kept a lot of our things safe besides giving us a place to sit.

Instead of paper, Mama used any kind of towels, sheets, pillowcases or whatever we could spare to wrap all these things, which was a lot more valuable to us later than paper would have been. A lot of these tips came from our Uncle Sepp who lived in Schweinfurt, which had already been bombed severely several times. His bicycle shop had been destroyed and his home behind it heavily damaged, but one room had survived enough that they could live in it. They just had to climb through piles of rubble to get to it. He realized how much he had lost and how much he might have been able to save, if only he had been better prepared.

Mama heeded all of his advice gladly—it was after all the voice of experience. It was eerily accurate, almost like he had a premonition. Forget about suitcases he would say, if you are fleeing a burning house and climbing over rubble, you need your hands free. Every family member needs a rucksack or backpack filled with their personal needs, such as a change of clothing, underwear, socks or stockings, wash cloths and a towel and even a set of our real silverware. And everyone should have a blanket to be draped over the head and body to protect from falling sparks if we have to walk through fire. It all sounded very scary, but it all made sense and was very important for our survival, which was the uppermost thing on our mind at this time.

Of course, one couldn't just go out and buy backpacks—none were available—so Mama figured out how to sew some herself. All those discarded old winter coats and clothes that Mama had collected through the years and had us take apart at the seams, came in handy now. Some of that stuff had been stored in those crates up in the attic and actually they made terrific backpacks for all of us. Then she took it one step further and created two big bags with handles for Karin and me to store all our dolls in, along with all their beautiful clothes. Our lovely doll clothes closet we had gotten for Christmas never did get any use at all, as everything was packed up and stored in the basement. Even our big closet was mostly empty now as we were living out of our backpacks.

Our Sunday coats and dresses were draped over the large sewer pipe that ran across the end of the bomb shelter in the corner by the breakthrough. We had bags and other things stuffed under, around and on top of the huge pipe. Since the closet was almost empty, Uncle Sepp suggested we dismantle it because it was blocking the door to the hallway. It's always a good idea to have another exit in case the other one gets blocked, he said, and jumping out the window was not an option since we lived high up on the third floor. What was left in the closet was mostly more of Mama's rags that had been in the crates, so we had to move them again. This time we stuck them on top of the potato bins, which were getting close to being empty, for lack of a better place. So they too survived and came in handy later on.

Mostly we stayed close to home now as the thought of being caught somewhere without a bomb shelter was simply too terrifying to contemplate. Of course, there were public shelters throughout the city, which were clearly marked, but we were familiar with ours. Grabbing our backpack and running downstairs to the basement was almost a routine now (except when I couldn't wake up). But the alerts came earlier in the evening now, before we ever went to bed and they lasted longer.

Even our beloved visits with Tante Marie on Sunday afternoon were becoming rarer because the long stretch of open highway with no shelter or protection seemed too risky and dangerous. Our Sunday afternoon delight was now for the whole family to play Rummy, a new game for us, which we played with two decks of cards at the living room table. Karola would bring home a "date" or a girlfriend and sometimes they would also be included in our Rummy games. There really wasn't much to do for young people of dating age. There was no dancing, no bars, and movie houses played the same movie for weeks on end and were often interrupted by trips to the bomb shelter. It seemed like the word "fun" had been stricken from our vocabulary, everything was much too grim and serious.

One good thing happened in all of this, though. I was deemed smart enough to go to "Hauptschule," much to my relief. And like Karin, I really liked school now. Karin and I actually shared a classroom and some of our teachers, only at different times as we had shifts now. She would go in the morning and I in the afternoon, and vice versa. Nobody had all mornings or all afternoons. We would switch off to make it fair.

For once I had a teacher, Frl. Brendel who really seemed to like me. She would actually single me out to let me help her with little things, which almost embarrassed me a little bit, because I was so terribly shy and my self esteem had been squashed so many times before. It sure made me feel good though! Unfortunately, it only lasted about four or five months because sometime in January 1945 all the schools were closed permanently. I can't remember if we even went back after Christmas vacation. If we did, we didn't go for very long.

The reason given was that the children were just too tired to learn, since we spent every single night now in the bomb shelters. It really did take its toll on everyone, not enough rest, not enough food and living in fear all the time. It was tough for the adults as well as the children, no doubt. But people suspected the real reason for the school closings was that more room was needed for all the casualties pouring in from both fronts.

Young women with very small children were actually encouraged to try and find refuge with friends or family out in the villages because they would be safer there. At the same time they were admonished not to try and hang onto their apartments in town as they were needed for all the refugees pouring into Wurzburg. It was actually against the law to do so.

Mama, who had school age children, had to work—it was mandatory. It was only the women with babies who were excused from working. Mama's job was making plaster of Paris bandages and other bandages and she was working in a converted dancehall with a big stage for the orchestra, which evoked memories of countless fancy balls that had taken place there. We often wondered if those kinds of things were gone forever and if life would ever be the same again.

Our cousin Karola also worked at this place and Mama and Karola became closer than ever before, going back and forth to work together and sometimes Karola would spend a night at our house. Her husband Arthur was stationed at Schweinfurt where he was training new recruits and he was actually there during all the bombings and had to help with the clean-up afterwards, so he had already experienced the terrible destruction these bombings caused. He was terribly worried that the same fate would someday soon befall Wurzburg.

It spite of that, they felt very lucky that Arthur was still so close to home and they were able to see each other pretty often. Very few young couples were in that position and they were on cloud nine when Karola finally conceived and they were really looking forward to the birth of their baby. It was a difficult pregnancy in the end and Karola had to stop working at the bandage factory sooner than expected, when the baby was born one month early and feet first. This was in February 1944. The baby, whom they named "Marita" was not well and had to go to the children's hospital for a few weeks before they could bring her home.

By that time, Arthur had been transferred far away to the Eastern Front, close to the Russian border near a city named Breslau, which isn't even German anymore. I believe Poland is claiming it now. He was now training 65 year-old men who, along with fourteen-year-old boys had recently all been drafted. To him, it was far more difficult to train these old men, than the young recruits he was used to training. I don't know if he ever got to hold his little girl, but she certainly was on his mind.

He was a diligent letter writer and Karola saved every last one of them—a real treasure for Marita to this day. He so desperately wanted to see her; they were working on plans for Karola and Marita to travel by train to spend Christmas 1944 with him. But it was just impossible. The trains were few and far between and were terribly overcrowded, and were being bombed regularly. There were no hotels available, nor milk or baby food and other needs. The Russians were advancing rapidly and eventually completely surrounded the city of Breslau.

His very last letter to her was written two days before Marita's first birthday. He had been wounded but was getting ready to go back to the front in a few days. The very last words he ever wrote were asking about Marita, "Is she walking yet?" Years later the Red Cross told Karola the whole story. The Russians had overwhelmed the whole city, invaded all the hospitals and shot all the wounded men point blank, like sitting ducks. Arthur was buried in Breslau, most likely in a mass grave.

Arthur was barely twenty-eight years old at the time of his tragic death. More than fifty years later, I had the privilege of reading all of his letters into a tape recorder for Marita, his only child, who grew up in America and never learned to read German, especially not the old way of German writing, that I had learned my first three years in school. There were sixty-six letters, enough to fill six 90-minute tapes, all offering a fascinating glimpse into the past.

Marita had found these letters after her mother's death and more than twenty years had gone by since that time, when she asked me to read them for her. Like all children, she longed to know more about the father she never got to know, but who obviously adored her when she was a baby. I have to say that I had mixed feelings about it, feeling intrusive, if not voyeuristic, and at the same time being quite intrigued and honored by it. Much to my relief, there was not one embarrassing thing in any of those letters, just normal every day conversation of two people desperately struggling to have some semblance of a "normal" life together.

They had created a lovely little apartment out of two of Tante Marie's six rooms in the little house in the "Kirschbaum," consisting of a beautiful bedroom suite with a cozy sitting area with two easy chairs and a radio, nice drapes too, and a very nice kitchen. Little did we realize how difficult it was to obtain all these things back then, the endless applications they had to fill out, and the lines they had to wait in just to get permission to buy something based on need, of course. Having permission however, didn't mean that anything was available to buy. In this case, it helped to know somebody who knew somebody and so on.

Arthur was very good at cultivating "connections," but even then it took months just to find a kitchen stove and a kitchen cabinet and a table and some chairs. Many of his early letters concern themselves with that very subject. Later, as the war dragged on and he was transferred far away from home, his letters turned much more nostalgic as he was wishing with all his heart to have a normal life with a normal job that would allow him to come home in the evening to enjoy his place and his family. Unfortunately, it never happened.

At the same time, our Aunt Hanni, who had gotten married a year after Karola was also searching for a place of her own. She was still living with her parents, our Oma and Opa, but after her little boy, our cousin Heinz was born, it was getting pretty cramped there. Then Tante Marie (her sister) learned of an apartment that became available in the big house in the "Kirschbaum" and encouraged Hanni to grab it. Of course, Hanni had the same problem as Karola—no furniture.

Luckily, after serving her time in the Arbeitsdienst, Hanni had been working as a mailman for a while, getting to know a lot of people, one of whom knew where she could get some used furniture. This was the time when all the attics had to be cleaned out to eliminate fire hazards in case of air raids. When the Jewish people had to leave, a lot of their furniture was stored in attics, in case they came back. Of course all that had to come out now and Hanni was able to buy some of it.

It was big, heavy old-fashioned dark furniture, the kind antique dealers would drool over now, and Helm, her husband, didn't like it at all, but Hanni was very proud of it. She was also checking the paper every day for a used stove and finally found one, a rotten looking thing that someone had painted green, but the heat had turned the paint brown. She worked on it with pot scrubbers and scouring powder for weeks until it looked presentable and then hauled it up the hill and to the Kirschbaum in Opa's Leiterwagen (cart). Then she had to stand in line to apply for permission to hunt for and buy stove pipes because no used ones were available. Apparently used things didn't need permission, but it was extremely hard to come by.

Hanni ended up with two big rooms, a bedroom and a living room and a small kitchen. She used her bridal veil to make curtains for the windows because nothing else was available by then. Besides, Hanni was much too practical to let all those beautiful yards of fabric go to waste.

Thirteen

It seems the winter of 1944 was colder than usual and it brought a lot more snow. I remember sloshing through tons of it on our way to Tante Marie's house for our annual New Year's Eve celebration. Of course, nothing in the world could have kept us from doing that, it was the highlight of the year for us after all, but this year we didn't really know what to expect.

Earlier, Mama and Tante Marie had even been talking about probably having to toast the New Year with "Linden-bluten tee," the tea made with the blossoms of the Linden trees, that Tante had taken a liking to since there was no "real" tea or coffee available and hadn't been for a long time. But lo and behold, somehow Mama came up with a small bottle of wine and so did Tante Marie, who even had a little bit of rum and black tea stashed away, just for this occasion, and together they brewed up just enough punch for everyone to get a good swallow to toast the New Year 1945.

Leading up to the big moment, we had been doing all the usual things, playing funny party games, bombarding each other with tiny, colorful paper balls, and dousing each other with confetti. Everyone was draped with the thin, colorful streamers called "shlangen," (snakes) that started out as rings, but when blown in the middle turned into beautiful spirals. For a little while, everyone tried to forget this endless, awful war we were in and just have some fun, but it was impossible not to think about the men who weren't there.

Uncle Willi, our cousin Karl and our cousins Betty and Karola's husbands Max, and Arthur all were fighting at the Russian Front in a bitter cold winter. Some hadn't been heard from in quite a while. Arthur's younger brother Fritz, who was also in Russia, had been reported "missing," and was probably captured. Hanni's husband Helm, who was "lucky" enough to be at the Western Front was wounded when a hand grenade one of the recruits tried to throw, exploded prematurely in his hand. It killed the recruit and wounded several others. Helm lost one of his eyes, but as a "professional" soldier, he had signed up for twelve years and a little thing like missing an eye wasn't getting him off the hook. He got a glass eye and went right back to his outfit at the Western Front.

Nobody knew if we would ever see any of these guys again or what shape they would be in if we did. All we could do was hope that this new year we were greeting would finally bring an end to all this madness. We had barely finished clinking our punch cups together, and shouting our "Prost Neu Jahr's" at midnight, when we suddenly heard strange, loud noises outside. We didn't know what they were, but Tante and her gang all had heard those sounds many times before. They told us it was the anti-aircraft artillery guns nearby, shooting at something unknown, since we hadn't even heard any planes at all. Apparently, sometimes they even hit something.

Only recently, our cousin Karola had been bending over her kitchen stove one evening trying to light a fire, her beautiful, faithful German Shepherd dog "Senta" whom Arthur and brought into the family, right by her side, when she noticed the dog growling and baring her teeth, ready to attack. Then she saw a man in a strange uniform, something like a flight suit, standing by the door. She said she couldn't tell who was more scared and startled—she of the man, or the man of the dog, but the man took off and disappeared into the night. No one knows what happened to him, but it was pretty safe to assume that he had jumped out of an airplane for one reason or another.

On this New Year's Eve, apparently the anti-aircraft artillery hit a bull's eye, as the next sound we heard was a horribly loud noise right above our heads. It sounded as if the whole roof was coming off, followed by a huge booming sound. Naturally, we all ran outside to see what was going on. All along, the snow had been falling silently and relentlessly, covering the barren landscape with a thick white blanket, but inside the barbed wire fence maybe 1500 feet or more past Tante's house, we could clearly see a burning airplane on the ground.

At first only the front seemed to be on fire and we thought we heard some faint screams, but soon the whole thing was engulfed in flames as we watched in horrified, helpless fascination. By the time the smell hit us, first of burning fuel and then the horrible stench of burning flesh, we noticed fire trucks and other activity outlined against the flames, but I'm sure it was too late for anyone to be saved. The realization that we had just witnessed the violent death of a human being, even if he was our enemy put an end to our celebration. No one felt like partying after that and even though we weren't a particularly superstitious bunch, we couldn't help but take this as a very bad omen for the coming year.

It kept on snowing right through the middle of January, which didn't really affect us that much in town. But up on the hill where Tante lived, the snow kept piling up until the road was all but impassable and she was completely snowed in, with no way to get supplies or even coal to heat at least one room or cook a meal. Finally the road was plowed enough so she could make her way to town and she came by our place to rest and warm up before making that long trek back and she told us about all that snow.

By then, Karin and I had been out of school for a while, going a little stir crazy and just dying to get out and play in the snow, of which there wasn't much in the city. In these uncertain times, Mama really preferred for us to stay close to home, but one day she did allow us to go up on the hill and visit Tante and see the snow. And it really was something to see! The long, lonely road was now just a narrow strip of white, with walls of snow on each side, taller than we were and it felt weird walking down that road, like walking through a very long tunnel. The air was very still and biting cold, not fun at all, but we made it to Tante's house, where another shock awaited us.

The house was so cold, due to the shortage of coal and wood and poor insulation, that we couldn't take our coats off. Every one there was bundled up like Eskimos, trying to keep from freezing to death, wearing woolen caps and mittens and overcoats in the house. What made this especially worrisome was the fact that besides the adults and Rudi, there were three babies in this cold house. There was Marita, not yet one year old and so tiny, every one called her "mouse," and there was Peterle, barely two and a half, and then there was Gertie, who was right in between the two.

This was a little boy, whose mother, coming from another town, appeared at Tante's doorstep one day, claiming this baby was Karl's son and she had no family and couldn't take care of him. Karl of course was in Russia by then, but Tante knew that he had been stationed near this woman's town briefly and that he had been dating someone there. Even though there was no way to prove it, Tante wanted to believe that this was her beloved son Karl's child—her grandson—and she took him in without hesitation. The mother went back to her previous life of which very little was known and she was rarely heard from after that.

Sadly, this turned out to be a big disappointment for poor Tante Marie. As the baby grew into a little boy, it became clear that there was absolutely no family resemblance at all in him—none of Karl's good looks or his sweet, easy-going manner that made Karl so loveable and attractive. This child was high-strung, prone to piercing screaming fits, not a happy child at all, in spite of Tante's best efforts to love him and care for him and tend to all his needs.

Now it was even tough to bring these children to town, as they all had to be pushed in baby carriages, an almost impossible task in this deep snow, so they just huddled together, trying to keep the kids from getting sick and longing for Spring. Somehow, everyone made it through January.

Then came February 4th, a cold, dreary, rainy Sunday, and much too nasty to go anywhere, so we stayed home, and played Rummy and other games. As far as the war was concerned, it had been mercifully quiet lately with not too many bomb alerts or bombings and we were full of hope that Wurzburg would be spared after all. On this Sunday evening Mama was in the kitchen fixing supper.

Papa and Karin were playing a game for two people, called "Muhle," and I was sitting on top of the table watching intently, as I hadn't quite mastered this game yet and Karin was always beating me at it. Suddenly, without any warning at all, a huge, loud "whoosh" came over our roof, much like the one on New Year's Eve, only this one was so powerful, it blew the windows open or shattered them (I don't remember which), and knocked all three of us away from the table and into the next room where we found ourselves in a tangled heap on the floor. Nobody was hurt too badly, just a little bruised and shook up.

Later we learned that it was a stray bomb that had come over our roof, and grazed the old Lion's Bridge, just a stone's throw from our house. It knocked a chunk out of the stone railing of the bridge and landed in the river—luckily for us! Several other "stray" bombs had been released at the same time, causing much damage and several fatalities. The very next day more stray bombs fell on the city, again without any warning being sounded, catching people completely off guard and causing a lot of fatalities and a lot of damage.

Until then, everyone had relied on the sirens to warn them when it was time to go to the bomb shelter, but since they had proven to be so unreliable, a lot of people now headed for the shelters in the evening even before the sirens sounded. This was especially true of people who had to go to public shelters some distance from where they lived. Among those people were Tante Marie and her gang.

The recent bombings had been coming ever closer to the airstrip of the German Luftwaffe next to which Tante lived, so she felt very vulnerable, with no safe place to hide in at all. Her house had no basement and the big one next door was only half underground, which was no protection in case of bombings. The closest public shelter, called a bunker, was underneath the beautiful Hofgarten behind the Residenz, a good two and a half miles from Tante's house and this, more or less, became their second home.

The snow had finally melted enough so that the street was passable again, so every afternoon they would pack the kids into the carriages along with supplies and head for the shelter to spend the night. There were cots set up for people to sleep on, but the place was cold and dank, far from ideal and very unhealthy. But walking home in the middle of the night in a pitch dark city with all those little kids was also not a good option, so they were thankful that they were allowed to stay even after the "all clear" was sounded. Of course in the morning they still faced that long, cold, windy walk home and a cold, dank house when they got there.

Mama would have loved to take them all in, but they knew how cramped for space we were ourselves and they really wanted to go home to check on mail from Russia, change the kids' clothes, take care of the dog, and try to have some semblance of a normal life. For the sake of the "little mouse" Marita, the most vulnerable of the clan, Karola eventually did more or less move in with us. That is, she would spend her days with us and in the evening she would go to the bunker to meet her family, mostly because there wasn't enough room in our bomb shelter for Marita's baby carriage, where she slept.

Along with all the necessary gear and paraphernalia, Karola also brought her two love birds in their cage, a wedding gift from Arthur, that were on the verge of freezing to death as well. And best of all, she brought her big, beautiful radio. I don't know how she was able to bring all that stuff all that distance down the hill in the cold weather to our place, but it was wonderful to have a radio in the house.

Of course, we still didn't have electricity, but Mama had an arrangement with Frau Bitter next door to let us use one of her outlets by means of a very long extension cord we tossed out the window down to a small terrace next to Frau Bitter's bedroom. It wasn't exactly ideal and sometimes downright aggravating, as the cord had a habit of mysteriously becoming unplugged a lot, so we would have to run over there and ask to have it plugged in again. At the same time, it opened a whole new world to us, full of music and information and of course a large amount of propaganda too.

The one and only daily newspaper had shrunk to just two sheets and was nothing but a "mouthpiece" for the Nazi party, full of propaganda and constant admonishments to conserve coal and food (as if we had any to waste!) and the ever growing death lists honoring all the fallen heroes of Wurzburg and the surrounding area. Now with Karola's radio, it was possible to find out how the war really was going by listening to the "enemy station" late at night.

This of course was forbidden and actually punishable by death, which made it that much more spine tingling and exciting to huddle around the radio and listen to far-away voices with strange accents speaking of lost battles, defeat and the unspeakable suffering of the German soldiers, at the same time trying to give us hope that it would soon all be over, which in itself also sounded ominous and scary. Often it would be interrupted by jamming and squeaking noises or it would go off the air abruptly and always Mama would caution us never to tell anyone what we were doing. Obviously, things were absolutely horrible at both fronts and they weren't exactly rosy at home either, and going from bad to worse all the time.

Mama would wrack her brain trying to come up with tasty, nutritious meals for us, a hard thing to do when all she had to work with was potatoes and none of the good stuff (like butter) that makes them taste good. One time Frau Dehler gave her a recipe for some kind of different potato dumplings with a meatless, fatless gravy flavored with thyme and soon after that, everything we ate had a hint of thyme in it. It filled our stomachs and kept us alive, but to this day I just don't care for the taste of thyme. I guess Mama liked it.

Laundry was another big problem as even soap powder was precious and hard to come by as was soap for bathing. Spending so much time underground, we were starting to feel like cave people, and taking our clothes off at any time seemed risky as it meant taking a chance on being caught with "our pants down" when we had to make a mad dash to the basement. But every so often we would take that chance, quickly wash up and change into some fresh, clean clothes to feel halfway human again. Since we didn't have a lot of spare clothes, everything we took off had to be washed pretty quickly and dried, which usually took several days and then put back into our backpacks for safe keeping.

It was shortly after the bomb landed in the river that it was once again time to do the laundry. As always, Mama had heated a big pot of water on the stove for that purpose, but when she picked up the pot to pour the water into the washtub the handle broke and all that scalding hot water poured over both her feet. I was in the kitchen with her watching the whole thing in horror and disbelief.

Karin and cousin Karola who had been in the living room, came running when they heard Mama's screams. We all helped her into the living room and took her slippers off and her stockings, with Mama moaning and crying and trembling from all the pain. Seeing her in so much pain and agony and not really being able to make it better was the absolute worst thing ever. We gently dabbed at her feet to get the water off and we fanned then to try and cool them, but that didn't do much good. Mama suffered terribly.

When the pain finally subsided somewhat, huge blisters appeared everywhere and the arches of both feet were filled with blisters as big as fists—just incredible. Mama couldn't believe that such a ridiculous thing would happen to her and she was actually angry with herself. Here we were in the middle of winter and it was very cold, and we had to be prepared to run to the bomb shelter three flights of stairs down below at any moment and Mama couldn't wear shoes or even walk. What a predicament!

Staying upstairs during a bomb alert was far too dangerous and not an option at all, so she wrapped her feet in bandages and slipped some of Papa's big grey wool socks over that and that is how she hobbled down to the basement on the edges of her feet. Then the rains came and the ceiling in the living room started dripping so we had buckets everywhere.

Next thing you know, large chunks of the ceiling came down, exposing all the ugly underpinnings up there, smelling wet and musty. The land lady wouldn't do anything as usual so Mama with her sore feet wearing Papa's socks and walking on the edges of her feet, climbed up in the attic along with Karin and me to see what was going on up there. That's when we discovered that the bomb that landed in the Main River hadn't been so kind after all, as it took part of our roof with it, leaving a gaping hole directly over our living room. Luckily, the wooden slats that held the red clay tiles in place were still there and we found a stack of new tiles in a corner.

Meanwhile, our cousin Karola had also climbed into the attic, so the four of us proceed to cover most of the big hole all in the pouring rain, with Mama wearing a babushka to keep her head dry and some of Papa's long underwear to keep her legs warm, because the stockings wouldn't fit over her blistered feet, and ladies didn't own pants then. She was a sight to see! But relief was immediate and no more rain was coming in, or at least very little. Of course, the damage had been done down below and there was no way we could repair our ceiling. It was kind of creepy to have all that plaster missing up there and even though the holes didn't go all the way through, it felt like someone could come down from there any minute.

Karin was totally freaked out about it and refused to sleep in that room. The only place she felt half way safe was in Mama's bed next to Mama. She couldn't sleep anywhere else and even then she slept fitfully and woke up at the slightest noise. It really wasn't just the ceiling but all the recent shocking happenings that were taking a toll on Karin's nervous system. A lot of people were affected that way and those that could, moved away from the city, including my accordion teacher, but we had nowhere else to go and all our relatives lived in Wurzburg and were in the same boat.

Mama was actually pretty stoic and calm about the whole thing and full of optimism. She would tell us "we'll be with the great majority," which I didn't really understand what that meant, but I thought it meant "we will survive," which was good enough for me (and obviously she was right!). We were as prepared as we could possibly be and the rest was up to God, our lives were in his hands. That doesn't mean that we didn't have doubts sometimes and wondered what horrors were yet to come our way, as we sat in the basement night after night with bombs falling on different parts of the city almost every night.

So far it only affected small areas each time, some uncomfortably close to home, but in spite of all the preparations, the death toll was horrendous. We learned that the best bomb shelter in the world was no protection at all if a very heavy bomb hit it directly, as was evidenced by one house where twenty-one people lost their lives as they huddled together in the basement. Then there were those that weren't hit at all, but the tremendous pressure of an exploding bomb would tear their bodies apart. All of a sudden, our basement didn't feel like such a safe haven anymore after all, but it still was our best chance of survival. What was happening to us now, had already happened to city after city all across Germany.

There would be a series of "mini-bombings" over a period of time all leading up to one giant, all-out, totally destructive and devastating bombardment, leaving not one building intact anywhere around. This is what everybody felt was coming and there was no escape from it. We were "in" for it, we just didn't know when. People were even more convinced of this, after Dresden was bombed.

This was a beautiful old city, much like Wurzburg, with no war industry whatsoever, and a population of invalids, old people and children, very much like our town and yet it became the most completely destroyed city ever in one single night. It was overkill and totally incomprehensible. I don't know how many people lost their lives that night. The date was February 14th.

Fourteen

Another month went by of almost nightly bombings here and there, and each time we were afraid of "the big one" and relieved when it wasn't, and always hoping and praying that we would be spared. Then came March 16th, 1945—a day no one who lived through it will ever forget.

It had started out to be a beautiful spring day, the first one of the year. Some bakery in the neighborhood was baking bread, so Karin and I went and stood in line for a while and actually were lucky enough to get some. The schools were shut down so we had plenty of time to be outside and enjoy the sun. After being cooped up all winter, it was a wonderful feeling. Mama even let us put on knee-highs, a sure sign that spring was here after wearing long stockings and the "harness" that held them up all winter.

With our knees exposed, naturally we had to go downstairs to let them soak up some sunshine. The street was our playground, all we had to do was hang out a little while and soon we would be joined by a whole bunch of neighborhood kids. Traffic was no problem at all, since no one on our street owned a car. Even if they did, no gasoline was available for civilians, so they were useless. There were some strange looking cars that had been "retrofitted" with wood burning heaters that powered the engine, for those who just had to have a car, such as doctors who made house calls and so on, but they rarely came down our street.

Landwehr Strasse (our street) was unique in another way too, unlike all the other streets around us; it only had houses on one side. The upper part between Sanderstrasse and Reurergasse had houses on one side and the huge, forbidding church complex on the other. It was wide enough to even have a sidewalk. The lower, narrower part where we lived stretched from Reurergasse down to the Kasern with a long row of houses on the same side as the church and a very tall long wall covering that same distance on the opposite side. Some kind of a medieval looking gateway reached from the church over to the wall, thereby visually separating the upper from the lower part, which seemed to be its only function.

Every one knew that behind this wall lay a huge garden that reached almost to the Lion's Bridge where the "brothers" from the church grew enough vegetables and other things to supply all the other brothers and probably the nuns and the priests too. The fact that the wall was so solid and so tall, that there was no way to peek in there, lent a certain air of mystery to the place. Even from our third floor windows, we could only see a small part of the far side, where we would see some monks working sometimes. But, we couldn't figure out how they got in there.

There was a very tall, solid, heavy wooden gate in the wall just two houses down from us across from the guesthouse, but it was almost always locked from the inside. Only when someone picked up a load of vegetables would it be ajar for a few minutes, but we were shooed away from it then. It was a wonderful place to bounce balls up against and play games such as the German version of Red Rover, and other games.

Having no houses to face across the street definitely made our neighborhood much more private and less noisy and we liked that a lot. On this beautiful spring day when we were at last able to spend a little time outside once again, it almost seemed like old times to us, except our best friends, the Pfaff twins had apparently found shelter with relatives outside Wurzburg and we missed them.

Papa, who seemed to be working all the time now, had to go on night shift (again!). Karola, our cousin, had left with Marita to go to the bunker. Karola, our sister, had a "date" with a young soldier she had met by chance, who was to report back to his unit the next day, after having been wounded and recovering in a Wurzburg hospital, far from his home in the Rheinland. She didn't really feel like going at all, but she felt sorry for him, being so lonesome and having to go back to the war the next day, so with Mama's encouragement and approval she left, but she was only going to stay a little while.

At seven o'clock, just like clockwork, the "coffee grinder" flew over, an almost nightly occurrence. This was some kind of reconnaissance plane with a very distinctive sound, ergo the name. Blaring sirens for a bomb alert followed just a few minutes later, and this evening was no exception. About fifteen minutes after the coffee grinder flew over, the sirens sounded and it was time to grab our bags and head for the basement, as we had done so many times before. This was actually the 335th air raid alert since the war began, not counting all the surprise bombings when no alert was sounded.

Besides various bags and back packs, Mama even grabbed the small laundry basket full of bread we had been hoarding, whenever we could get our hands on some and a bowl with eggs she had been lucky enough to be able to buy, all very precious things in these times of very short rations and almost constant hunger. We couldn't leave all that upstairs! Her feet though, were still tender and had healed enough that she could wear shoes again.

In the basement, everybody who was assigned to it (about 19 people) was present and accounted for, except for Karola, and Mama really fretted about that now. All we could hope for was that she had found a safe public shelter somewhere else.

At first it was deadly quiet as we all just sat and waited, lost in our own thoughts. But once the bombing started every one knew that this was the real thing, no "boom-pow-crash-bang" here and there like before. This was a constant, horrendously terrifying rain of bombs, like we had never heard before, so loud that it made our eardrums pop. Some of the children were screaming, some women were praying loudly, trying to be heard above the horrible noise of the falling bombs.

The dim light bulb flickered on and off, leaving us in total darkness at times, while the so called "safe" freezer locker door had been ripped out of its latch and was now flapping wildly back and forth. One of the older boys tried to lock it back and nearly had his shoulder dislocated from the tremendous pressure created by the falling bombs. We just wanted everything to stop, but it seemed to go on and on forever. Actually it was only twenty terrifying minutes, but it seemed more like two hours.

Finally, it appeared that the bombing had ended, but other really scary sounds emerged such as things exploding and crashing to the ground. We were waiting for the "all clear" siren that would tell us that it was now safe to leave the shelter, but it never came. At least, we never heard it. Without the all clear, a second wave of bombers could have been heading our way to hit us again, so it was risky to leave. Then the acrid smell of smoke started to creep into the basement.

Mama carefully opened the door of the crawl-through we were sitting next to, not knowing what to expect, but not really expecting to see much, because the escape window had had a protective lean-to cover built over it. But apparently the cover had been blown away and an ominous red glow could be seen through the window. The oldest two boys in the basement, Hansi Bitter and Max Altenhofer, both not quite fourteen yet, acting very brave and manly, volunteered to go upstairs to check things out in spite of no "all clear" signal. They were back in no time, excitedly confirming what Mama already knew, that everything was on fire and we would all burn to death if we didn't get out right away, almost creating a small panic.

Everyone jumped up and headed for the door at the same time, the ones who had been closest to the door were the first ones out of course. We who had been banished to the back corner had to wait for everyone else to get out of the way. Mama handed me my back pack while people all around me were rushing toward the exit. Usually she helped me put it on my back, but she couldn't get to me so I just held it by the straps along with my blanket.

I was absolutely terrified of being left behind in the dark basement. When I saw the last pair of legs disappearing at the top of the stairs, I scrambled up after them, thinking Mama and Karin would be right behind me. Somehow there seemed to be safety in numbers, but it was just as scary upstairs.

The normally very dark street was now bathed in an eerie red glow. The sky was blood red and there was a strange, loud roar in the air as a firestorm was forming. It was hot and oppressive, making it hard to breathe. Sparks were flying down like rain and there was debris everywhere. The Kaserne at the end of Landwehr Strasse was engulfed in flames. Some people had tried to make their way to the Main River that way, but they were driven back by the intense fire.Our only escape would be Sanderstrasse at the other end, so everyone was running in that direction.

With my eyes on the fleeing crowd, I tripped over a big beam that was lying in the middle of the street and dropped my back pack, but I was in such a panic that I just left it there and kept on running. I got as far as the medieval gate when people were coming back from the upper part of Landwehrstrasse. There was no escape that way either, as a huge pile of fiercely burning rubble from the completely destroyed four story corner house blocked the intersection there. We were trapped like rats!

Our last resort was the narrow Reurergasse, where all the houses were on fire and visibility was zero because of the thick, black smoke. It was extremely dangerous and frightening, but I guess everybody went that way, because all of a sudden I was all alone standing at the corner not knowing what to do. Meanwhile, Mama was still in the basement desperately groping around searching for something, with Karin by her side pleading with her to get out of there.

Finally Karin realized what Mama was searching for—Karola's handbag. Karin had been holding onto Mama's arm all along, so together they made their way up Landwehrstrasse with Mama shouting my name all the way. She was hoarse when we found each other and I was never happier in my life to see two people than when Mama and Karin appeared out of the smoke. Of course, even in this dire situation I had to face the music right away.

First of all, for running out on Mama and Karin, I have felt guilty about that all my life and do to this day, even though they are both long gone now, and they probably forgave me. Second, I was read the riot act for losing my backpack, which contained all my worldly possessions. Mama actually contemplated going back to get it, weighing all her options—should she go alone and leave us there at the corner, not knowing if she would make it back, or should we all go and risk perishing in the street together.

In the end, common sense prevailed and she forgot about the backpack—it was much more important now to save our lives. This meant heading down that scary Reurergasse, which now also seemed to be partially blocked by fire, but before we got to that point, Mama noticed a sign for a public shelter beneath the Reurer Church and this is where we found refuge for a while. It was a tremendous relief to get away from the fire and the smoke, but to say it was wonderful would be wildly exaggerating.

The place was so crowded we could barely get in the door. It was also completely pitch dark, so we could only sense people all around us. There was about an inch of water on the floor from the emergency toilets overflowing, so we couldn't set down any of the bags Mama and Karin were carrying (probably Karola's and Papa's backpacks besides their own), and there was absolutely no place to sit at all. We just stood there in the dark, holding onto each other, so we wouldn't get separated again.

Every so often someone would try to light a candle, giving us a quick glimpse of the incredible amount of people that were packed into this place, but the candle would always go out again right away, or maybe it was the match. Apparently, the oxygen level was so low that a match wouldn't burn. It was getting harder and harder to breathe, making it only a matter of time before everyone would suffocate.

The whole situation was so unreal that we lost all sense of time and I have no idea how long we were in that shelter, but I know the thought of having to go back out into that inferno was absolutely terrifying, yet it was our only chance for survival. Some official sounding young women with flashlights who had come out of nowhere made that abundantly clear to everyone. They also said not to be afraid, they would lead us to safety, one small group at a time, sounding very reassuring.

When it was our turn, Mama had me up front with Karin right behind, so I was the first one out the door and came face to face with a wall of fire just a few steps above me. I just froze, since there was no way was I going to be able to go up those stairs! That's when one of the young women stepped between me and the fire and another one grabbed my hand and led me down a narrow passageway that I hadn't even noticed with everyone following behind.

The long, dark hallway literally had a light at the end of the tunnel, but it was flickering like flames and my heart just sank, thinking we would have to walk through fire after all, but when we turned the corner, it was a tall candlestick with an altar candle lighting the way. We took a few more turns, another hallway, up some stairs, across a narrow walkway, through a creaking old door and we found ourselves at the top of a curving stone staircase leading down into the "mysterious" garden. So that's how the brothers got in there!

The "medieval gate" was actually a passageway over Landwehrstrasse, from the church to the garden, and we never knew that. The garden wasn't so mysterious either, just rows upon rows of very neat beds for growing things with sandy walkways in between. The young woman led us about halfway to the other side of the garden and then showed us a gate where we could get out and make our way to the Lions Bridge, while she hurried back to help another group.

To us, those courageous women were angels sent from God. They were definitely heroes who saved hundreds of lives, maybe even thousands as not one life was lost in the Reurerkirche bomb shelter. We never learned who they were or where they came from. It would be many years later before we learned exactly what happened that night.

According to my "Wurzburg Chronic" book, it was about 280 twin-engine British "Marauders" or "Mosquitoes" that dropped between 360,000 to 380,000 three-foot long stick incendiary bombs, along with about 220 explosive bombs each weighing 1000 pounds and an unknown amount of phosphorous "jelly" which oozes and burns seemingly forever and cannot be extinguished. This actually made some houses burn from the ground up, where most of them, of course, burned from the top down from the sheer volume of the incendiary bombs. It was estimated that there was one stick bomb per every two square yards of city area. So many hit the pavement and got stuck there protruding about six inches out of the ground, which people would later trip over constantly.

Our beautiful, picturesque Wurzburg with its very old houses and narrow streets and tiny courtyards full of charm, and so much more, was doomed and nothing could save it. Initially there were some heroic efforts by the fire department and volunteers in different areas to fight the flames, but it was completely futile and in the end they all had to run for their lives. Even the huge water reservoirs the city had dug in front of the main post office and other big squares around town for this kind of disaster were no match and went largely unused because the fire was too widespread, fast moving, and totally overwhelming.

In unexpected ways they did save lives though, as some people who were completely surrounded by fire, had no other choice but to jump into the reservoir and spend the night there with sparks raining down and smoke choking their lungs and burning their eyes. Everyone who survived that night has their own harrowing story to tell of absolute terror, heartbreak, and narrow escapes.

Exactly how many didn't make it has never been established. It was somewhere in the 5,000 range, a relatively small number considering the total population in this small space and the complete and total destruction of it. Only 2% of the buildings around the outskirts survived halfway intact, while 98% was either completely destroyed outright or so heavily damaged to be uninhabitable—burnt out and a total loss.

We matched and surpassed the destruction of Dresden, a dubious record nobody wanted or deserved. Surprisingly, in spite of the massive bombing, not too many people were killed by the falling bombs or debris. The majority of them died from suffocation, as they were too afraid of the fire and thought they would be safer in a bomb shelter. This of course would have been our fate too, if it hadn't been for those brave women who helped us and showed us the way to safety.

Once we reached the Lions Bridge, we definitely felt a lot better and we knew that we would be all right. Then we met the whole Bitter family who apparently had also been in the church bomb shelter and we even had to smile a little bit at sweet old Herr Seemann's expense. He was wearing a very elegant, expensive sable coat that Frau Altenhofer had been working on and someone had hung around his shoulders as he left our basement, and he was wearing a babushka over his cap to keep his ears warm. He could have been mistaken for a cute little old lady with soulful eyes, if it hadn't been for his huge, bushy walrus-type mustache. After what we had just been through, it was so good to have something to smile about, and I don't think he minded at all.

At the same time we also found one of the Altenhofer's boys, nine-year-old Karlemann, who was trying hard not to cry because he couldn't find any of his family and was totally lost. We consoled him and told him to stay with us and in the morning we would find his mama. It got really cold that night, as we sat on a blanket by the Main River, where in happier times we had picnicked with our dolls. Karin and I were wishing we had never taken our long stockings off.

All around us were fellow survivors like us who had been lucky enough to escape the inferno. Up an incline and across a broad tree-lined avenue, we could see a huge apartment building being consumed by flames, section by section. A section would burn fiercely for a while and come crashing down with a tremendous noise and the fire would immediately jump to the next section. It was sad and yet fascinating to watch, and somehow we knew that life would never be the same again.

Next morning, Mama and Frau Bitter decided to try and check things out, leaving Herr Seemann there to keep a watchful eye out for all of us kids. After a while, they came back with bad news and good news. Landwehrstrasse was buried under tons of debris and all the houses were nothing but smoldering piles of rubble, but Papa was alive and as well as could be expected.

His workplace at the railroad had been smashed to pieces, but he made a harrowing escape from there. Then it took hours to get back to our neighborhood because every single street was blocked by fire. When he finally made it to the area, it was impossible to get to our house, so he stood on the Lions Bridge and watched everything he had worked so hard for turn to ashes. At the same time, he had no clue if any of us had survived. It really took its toll on Papa and it would be a long, long time before he could smile and sing and joke again the way he used to.

We were so glad when Mama told us that our Papa was all right. She had also found Frau Altenhofer at the rubble. They had had a falling out recently—probably due to some misunderstanding and terribly frayed nerves, and they hadn't been speaking to each other. But when they saw each other they fell into each other's arms and had a good cry together. Frau Altenhofer had lost track of two of her children, Max and Karlemann (of course we had Karlemann with us), and Mama was worried sick about Karola.

While they were still trying to console each other, Max and Karola came down the street together, climbing over all the debris, followed by Heinz, the soldier with whom Karola had had the date the night before. They had been walking along the Main River, when Karola noticed all these beautiful "Christmas trees" all lit up in a huge circle up in the sky, just suspended there looking gorgeous.

She was awestruck, wondering what they were, what did they mean, and where did they come from? Heinz knew exactly what they were and what they meant.

"This is how the enemy marks an area that is going to be bombed," he told her. "You've got about 15 minutes to get home."

They only did that sort of marking for an all-out bombardment involving a lot of airplanes, so he knew it would be really bad, most likely total devastation. Right about then, the sirens started blaring and Karola was so afraid that she wouldn't make it home before the bombs started falling. She and Heinz ducked into some sort of sheltered area underneath the street that led to the Lions Bridge. Even though this wasn't an official bomb shelter, a lot of people had done the same thing.

Karola met Max in the chaotic aftermath of the bombing. Apparently, he was one of the first ones to leave our basement and he was able to get to the river before the fire drove everyone else back. Together they fled across the Lions Bridge and spent the night in the vineyards, watching the whole city go up in flames from the hills across the river—a sight no one would ever forget.

Now, as we were sitting by the river cold, tired, hungry and miserable, all we wanted to do was go home. We had to go and see with our own eyes that this wasn't possible anymore and the best way to do that was through the Brother's garden. Miraculously, even though the wall was still standing everywhere else, it had collapsed in front of our house and the gate had burned away, making it a lot easier to get to our pile of rubble. Just about everyone from our shelter was now congregating around, and no one had eaten since the night before and no one knew what to do or where to go from here.

Some prison guards came by with two or three prisoners of war in tow—Frenchmen I believe. They came from the small prison (actually a converted gym) on Korngasse, the next street over. A corner of their yard had butted up against our backyard, but their yard was surrounded by very tall walls, so we never saw them. We would hear them singing over there and playing soccer sometimes, talking excitedly in a language we didn't understand. They were all homeless now too, since the whole neighborhood was destroyed, but they were going around offering a helping hand and rescue where needed.

Mama asked if it would be possible to go into the basement through the escape window, which was completely exposed since the lean-to had been blown away. So, one of the prisoners climbed down there, but he only went as far as the front part where the coal and potato bins were. The things Mama wanted were in the "safe room" which meant crawling through the breakthrough into pitch black darkness. Everyone refused to do that, saying it was too dangerous and impossible because there was no air down there—one would have to have a gas mask.

Well, as an assigned air raid warden, Mama was required to keep her gas mask with her at all times, so much to their surprise she produced her gas mask, but they still refused to go. Their job was to rescue people, not possessions, so Mama strapped on her gas mask and climbed down there and through the breakthrough herself. No one could stop her.

She had been so bitter about the "yucky" corner we had ended up with and now it was the greatest blessing as all our possessions were stashed around the breakthrough. All she had to do was feel around, grab whatever she could and hand it out the breakthrough where a human chain had formed. Everything we touched was so hot that it burned our fingers. Mama was working feverishly to get out as much as possible, because she knew she wouldn't last very long with that confining gas mask. It was very hard to breathe.

Some people, especially Herr Albert, the "communist" kept yelling for Mama to get some of their bags for them, which would have meant delving deeper into the hot, black abyss our basement had turned into. Mama knew better than to do that. In the end, she didn't have the strength left to crawl out of the breakthrough, she just leaned into it and two men pulled her out.

After a while, Herr Albert asked to borrow the gas mask so he could go down there himself, which Mama gladly let him have. He was down there only a very short time when he emerged carrying only one small bag and was obviously very shook up. He wanted to know who had been the last person to leave the basement the night before, which of course were Mama and Karin. Apparently, while groping around under his bed for the bag, he came across a human foot—at least that's what it felt like to him and he just grabbed his bag and hot tailed it out of there.

It turned out, the foot Herr Albert had held in his hand was attached to Frau Ohrlein from up the street, an elderly lady who was known for refusing to go to the bomb shelter at all cost. How she ended up in ours is anyone's guess. Most likely, she was trying to find refuge with her friend Frau Altenhofer (the elder one), when things got scary. But of course, everyone else had already left from there.

Obviously, the stairs were still clear when she went down there. It will never be known if the house collapsed while she was still conscious and she couldn't get out, or if she decided to rest a while and the smoke overwhelmed her. She died of suffocation. We didn't learn any of that until much later though.

No one else would go down there that day, so we weren't even sure if there was a body down there or not. Everyone scattered after that and most of the people we never saw again, including the Pfaff twins and all the other kids we used to play with and go to school with.

Mama thought Herr Albert was crazy, but boy was she glad she didn't go near that bed! She said if that had happened to her, she probably would have died of shock right there and if she had known that a dead body was down there, she might not have been able to make herself go in there. She was a tremendously courageous and tough woman in so many ways, but she was afraid of dead people.

Thank goodness we never saw any even as we made our way through the park and past piles and piles of smoldering and still burning rubble on our way to Tante's house. We didn't know what we would find there, but it was the only logical place for us to go. No one could live in the city at all, as the entire infrastructure had been destroyed.

There was no water, no gas, no electricity, and no stores to buy anything. All the streets were impassable because they were piled high with rubble, and there was no machinery to clear them with. Even hand tools were in short supply. People would sift through their rubble and find their tools melted from the intense fire, so there were mountains of rubble and no shovels for cleanup. Wurzburg became a dead city and everyone who had survived had to find some other place to live.

We had invited Heinz, the soldier, to join us for the time being, because the hospital and the place where he was supposed to report for duty were wiped out and he had no clue where else to go. Also, his extra pair of hands came in handy to help us carry our things. We felt incredibly lucky as we approached Tante's house loaded down with everything we had left in this world to find the two houses intact. They had survived the bombing. Of course, with six extra people, Tante's little house was bursting at the seams, but that wasn't the worst of it.

Soon we discovered that our enemy wasn't finished with us yet. Where the slower moving British Royal Air Force specialized in bombing cities at night, now it was the faster American's turn to bomb anything left standing and shoot at anything that moved in the daytime.

Any plane that landed at the airfield next to us was shot to pieces immediately. There were no more sirens and no safe place to hide. We were sitting ducks for the American air force. Our instincts told us to run at the first sound of an airplane, but there was no place to run to nearby.

One time, Karin and I were outside when we heard planes approaching. We tried to run down the highway to the little town of Gerbrunn, where someone had turned their root cellar into something like a bomb shelter, but the planes caught up with us and started shooting. They were so low that we could see the grinning faces of the pilots and all we could do was dive into the ditch alongside the highway. We were pinned there for a long time as they kept turning and flying over again and again, still shooting.

Karin nearly had a nervous breakdown after that. We were all shell-shocked and our nerves were frazzled. We felt totally vulnerable and maybe we weren't thinking too rationally at the time, but we decided that we couldn't stay there anymore because it was just too dangerous.

Karola, our cousin, for some reason or another knew a farmer's family in a little town named Euerdorf near Bad Kissingen, some thirty miles from Wurzburg. She suggested that maybe we could go there.

Well, anything sounded better than what we had, so it was worth checking out. Heinz knew how to operate Uncle Willi's motorcycle, so together they went and checked the place out. When they came back, they actually had found three rooms in Euerdorf, each one on a different street, but that didn't matter. Someone they knew with a big truck agreed to drive us there.

So we loaded up a bunch of furniture, mostly Karola's nice things. She had lost her radio and her lovebirds and all of the other things she had brought to our place, and she didn't want to lose anything else. By the time Tante piled her things onto the truck there was barely enough room left for us and our meager belongings. Some of our things we had to leave behind, such as our big bags full of dolls, which we locked in Hanni's basement next door.

Thankfully, she had survived too, along with Heinz, her little boy and her parents, our grandparents. She still has very vivid memories of that fateful night just like everyone else who lived through it. They were in a wine cellar converted to a bomb shelter below the restaurant "zum stern" next door when the bombing started. Some empty wine barrels that incredibly were stored near the entrance must have suffered a direct hit, turning that whole area into an inferno, leaving them no choice but to smash through the breakthrough wall to the house next door and somehow they found their way out of there.

Then she made a mad dash through the smoke-filled staircase up to our grandma's apartment to retrieve Heinz's baby carriage. She knew she would need that desperately as Heinz was too little to walk anywhere and too heavy to be carried. She saw our grandma's Sunday dress lying on the bed, so she grabbed it too and that is about all they rescued out of there.

Later they realized that our grandpa was wearing house slippers because he had forgotten to put on his shoes, so he didn't even have any shoes to wear. Together they made their way down Domstrasse trying to get to the river with a terrible firestorm brewing above them and burning cinders raining down on them, little Heinz screaming at the top of his lungs. Then Hanni realized that the pillow in the carriage was smoldering.

At the famous fountain down at the corner, they stopped for a moment and that is where she saw her dad break down and cry like a baby as the realization sank in that he had lost everything he had ever worked for. It was a heartbreaking moment for Hanni. No one likes to see their own dad in so much anguish that there is nothing left but tears. At the same time she didn't know if her own place was all right, but once she found that it was, she wasn't about to leave it again, so they stayed behind.

The rest of us, thirteen in all, piled into the truck on top of the furniture and wherever we could squeeze in for a harrowing trip along the outskirts of Wurzburg, past still fiercely burning factories, with nothing but devastation as far as the eye could see. All the while, we were watching the skies for approaching airplanes. Out on the highway it was even more dangerous as we would be clearly visible from above. One time we waited under a clump of trees for a while when a squadron of planes came over.

We safely made it to Euerdorf, which was a typical small German village. We had one small room with a big, wood-burning cook stove, and this became our kitchen. It was adjacent to a washroom, a "washkuche," where the owners did their "big" laundry once a month. It had a big wash kettle, some long tables and a bench, and most importantly, a big sink where we could get our water. This more or less became our living room. The toilet was right outside the door, behind another door and that is all there was—no sink or bathtub at all.

Two streets over we had another room, which became our bedroom for seven people, the rest slept in the kitchen. We were used to close quarters, but this was closer than even we were used to. The third room our cousin Karola and Heinz had rented was not really livable as there was no stove, no water or toilet, and it was upstairs with the "misthaufen," the pile of manure from cleaning out the cow barn right down below. This became a storage room for all the excess furniture Tante had brought.

One thing we noticed right away was that everyone in Euerdorf went about their business totally unconcerned with the planes flying over. It would take us years to get over the fear and the instinct to run for cover at the sound of an airplane. This village was largely untouched by the war and we could almost relax and breathe a little easier there and not fear for our lives all the time. But soon we found out that the people who rented rooms to us refugees, had also rented out their barns to the German Army for storage.

Incredibly, not long after we had settled in, the two areas where we had rooms were attacked by low flying planes, which set the barns on fire and caused quite a panic. Some stray bullets actually came through the ceiling of our bedroom and started a fire on the wooden floor. This happened in broad daylight when normally no one would have been there, but our Karola hadn't been feeling well and was asleep in the bed when she was rudely awakened by the bullets and was able to put out the fire. If not for her, the house might have burned down or at the very least our bedroom would have been destroyed, as everyone's attention was on the burning barn right behind the house.

The barn at the other house, where the furniture was stored, also burned to the ground but they were able to save the house. It was uncanny that those two buildings would be singled out and nothing else until we learned what they were being used for. Not many people knew that, but the fact that the enemy knew exactly what to destroy made it clear that there had to be a spy among us. A man in the next village just two kilometers away was suspected of being that spy and even being in radio contact with the enemy but nothing could ever be proven.

The fire in the barn actually turned out to be somewhat of a blessing for us. It had been full of food for the Army and most of it was destroyed but a small section of dried green peas and macaroni survived and the sergeant in charge told us to bring some bags and he would fill them up for us on the sly as it wasn't really his to give away. It was singed and completely permeated with smoke that no amount of rinsing and boiling could remove, making it taste terrible, but we just pretended that we were eating pea soup with ham in it. The same thing had happened to the bread we had rescued out of our basement, so we were already used to that awful taste. (The eggs, by the way, were almost soft boiled from the heat in the basement.)

We would always remember the kindness of this one man, a real "mensch," a human being with the compassion of which there was none forthcoming at all from the rich farmers in the village. We would go to the packed church for Sunday Mass wearing our blue Sunday coats singed with brown streaks and smelling from smoke that no amount of airing out could get out, and the priest would preach and ask the people to be kind and compassionate to us Wurzburgers who had been through hell, but all we got was cold stares and downright hostility.

We should have put the fire out, is what we were told time and time again. It's not like we wanted anything given to us, we would have gladly paid any price for some food, but they said they had none to spare. Mama had to beg to be able to buy a sack of potatoes to sustain us.

We had no bread to eat, but every Saturday morning we watched a parade of people heading for the bakery up the street with huge pizza-sized cakes on both hips to be baked at the bakery. The tradition of having cake on Sunday was alive and well in Eurerdorf, it just didn't include us. We got to smell the wonderful aroma that was wafting through the village and watch the parade in reverse when all those good things were being carried home right past our kitchen window.

Things really weren't all bad though for us kids. We had a beautiful spring, and the weather was gorgeous, so we spent most of our time outside exploring the area, which was actually very pretty and so peaceful that even Karin, who had been a bundle of nerves, started to relax. We loved to roam the lovely woods that smelled so fresh and fragrant, not smoky like Wurzburg. There was an abundance of wood lying around, which was good, as we needed some kind of fuel for our cook stove.

We would borrow a cart and it would take us no time to fill it up and haul it home. It was all so new to us that we didn't mind it at all, even if it might have been considered work. When we weren't busy doing that, we loved to run through the tall grass in the meadows along the Saale River, something that was forbidden in the parks of Wurzburg. Someone would shout "Take cover," and we would belly flop down into the soft grass, completely hidden from view and do that over and over, it was so much fun.

As we ventured a little further away from the village, we discovered an old stone quarry that we loved to climb around in, and a brand new bridge that spanned the river but was never completed. Instead of a straight road across, it had three very deep drainage holes and one would have to run down one side and climb up the other and do that three times to get across. Needless to say, it was completely useless as a bridge, but it held a strange fascination for Karin and me because it was so unusual. It also had no access roads—really strange!

There was a normal bridge at the edge of town that we had to cross to get to the woods and this was also the main thoroughfare to Bad Kissingen and the rest of the world. At the other side of the village a railroad bridge spanned this main road, which led to other villages and ultimately to Wurzburg. A huge bomb could clearly be seen up under the bridge that was to be exploded as the enemy approached. It was big enough to not only blow up the bridge but probably half the village as well. Our kitchen was not too far from the bridge and the bedroom only a little bit further.

Fifteen

I can't say exactly when the Americans came to Euerdorf, but according to my book, The Chronik, the first American tanks entered Wurzburg on April 1st, after almost nonstop bombing to smooth the way. They were met with fierce resistance by the few troops and militia and whatever else was left in Wurzburg—mostly old men who were ordered to defend the dead, broken city. They were hopelessly outnumbered, out of ammunition, and apparently out of luck as many more lives were lost for absolutely nothing.

By April 4th, it was all over and Wurzburg was firmly in the hands of the Americans. From there, they pushed on toward Euerdorf, meeting all sorts of resistance along the way. We could hear the sounds of the battle and the ominous rumbling of the tanks coming ever closer. A few bedraggled German soldiers had retreated all the way to Euerdorf, planning to make a stand and defend the town. They had no tanks, no cannons, nothing. It was ridiculous.

We had to be prepared for the bridge being blown up, and for gun fighting in the streets, so we fled to a cave behind the sawmill since there were no bomb shelters in Euerdorf. As it turned out, not one shot was fired as some unknown person met the Americans with a white flag and surrendered the town to them. The bomb didn't go off because of a faulty detonator, probably sabotaged.

The Americans might have just rolled through town and never stopped except someone blew up the one and only "normal" bridge across the river. So they set up camp on the meadow by the river, not far from the cave where we were hiding. We had no clue what was going on outside and didn't know when it would be safe to come out, so Papa sneaked out and made his way to our kitchen. The streets were deserted as everyone was hiding.

In our kitchen, he cowered under the window, peeking out over the sill as the powerful American tanks started to roar into the village one by one, with GI's walking along each side, their guns ready to fire. The tanks were so tall they could look straight into our kitchen and the walls of the old building were shaking and Papa's whole body started to vibrate from the noise in the air. It was an awesome experience for Papa. He even came eyeball to eyeball with one of the GI's and his heart nearly stopped, but the soldier just went on.

Eventually, Papa made his way back to the cave. Mama was worried sick the whole time he was gone because it took so long and we were so relieved when he got back and told us everything he had seen. We had been terribly worried that the Russians might get there first as we had heard horror stories of their brutality and rough treatment of the people they conquered. We were really curious as to what the Americans looked like and Papa, with a touch of humor, told us they had eyes and a nose and a mouth, all in the same places we did.

What he neglected to tell us was that they were all black, which would have made it even more interesting to us because we had never seen any black people at all. It also would have made it a lot more worrisome for Mama, as stories of women being raped and brutalized had preceded them in large numbers. Of course, once we left the cave we knew the occupying forces were black right away because there were nothing but black faces in the camp that we had to pass, but Mama told us not to look and just hurry by.

We had never heard of segregation, knew absolutely nothing about it, the whole concept was astounding to us. So many things were astounding to us about these Americans. Their sheer numbers for one, their incredible friendliness and "can-do" attitude and all the wonderful equipment they brought with them. It took them no time at all to build a pontoon bridge across the Saale River strong enough to move their heavy tanks across and soon the whole "black" camp had moved on, heading for Berlin where Hitler was still dreaming of winning the war.

It would take another month, until May 8th, when Germany surrendered unconditionally, but for us the war was over when the Americans came to our village. A "white" company moved in right behind the "blacks" and occupied the town and all the German men were required to report to the Americans and be checked out and lay down any weapons they owned. A very tight curfew was imposed and no one could be on the street after 6:00PM.

Since our bedroom was on a different street than our kitchen, this complicated our lives somewhat, as we weren't all that punctual about eating supper. But a girl we had befriended showed us a secret alleyway that was completely hidden from the road. We just had to dash across one road so we could get to our bedroom unseen by going down this alley, turn a few corners and then climb over a tall wall—a real spine-tingling adventure for us kids. Mama didn't like it though.

Guards were posted at all the roads and no one could leave or enter the town without a pass. We had to have a pass to go to the forest to gather wood for our stove. They even let us use their pontoon bridge for that purpose at first, but before long they had bridged the gap in the beautiful old stone bridge with lumber, a temporary solution that worked very well. Once that was in place, the pontoon bridge disappeared to be used further on I suppose, as the German Army in a last ditch, desperate attempt to slow down the advancing onslaught of troops had blown up virtually every bridge in Germany.

Everyone thought how ridiculous it was to blow up the bridge in the first place, when the Americans had already crossed the mighty Rhine River, the Saale was no more than a little stream compared to that. Later we learned that all the bridges in Wurzburg had also been blown up. It may have slowed things down somewhat but it didn't stop anything at all in the end.

We, along with a group of village kids, loved to "hang out" with the soldiers guarding the bridge. They were all so young and full of life and enthusiasm and they all had beautiful teeth. That was the most remarkable thing to us, as so many Germans had bad teeth. Karin even had already learned enough English that she could communicate somewhat. She was shy about it but they got a kick out of meeting a little German girl who could speak their language.

We were too shy and too proud to beg for anything, but one time one of the other kids got a piece of Dentyne gum from one of the soldiers, which he tore into little tiny pieces so everyone would get a taste. Then we all pretended that we were eating rice pudding with cinnamon, something we hadn't eaten in a very long time. Hunger was still our daily companion.

Sometimes we walked to Bad Kissingen more than five miles away (a two hour walk), because we knew of a store there that would sell us all the sauerkraut and German lettuce we could carry. I don't remember the formula anymore, but apparently they had more of one thing than the other. For every pound of one thing we could get two of the other and we had to buy them both or nothing at all. We hauled home a lot of sauerkraut and lettuce from there (another two hours back). We ended up boiling the lettuce like spinach as we had no dressing to make a salad.

We even discovered some herbal tea there that we could buy and we were so glad of that as we had been picking flowers in the meadow and drying them to make tea, but it didn't taste very good. It was really tough for Mama to know that the farmers would feed their excess milk to their hogs rather than sell some to us. She knew we were growing children and needed milk for our bones to grow properly, but all we had was tea or water. I don't think she ever got over her hatred of those selfish, heartless people.

The sauerkraut would have tasted a lot better with some meat or fat in it, but we hadn't had any of that in a long time either. Papa was so sick of it that one day he just left with Mama's big brown leather shopping bag, saying he was going "hunting" to find us some meat. Everyone chuckled and laughed about that, but after a while he came back with a great big smile on his face, the shopping bag half full of meat.

Somehow he had found his way to the old quarry where he saw an American tank dumping something. After it left, he went to see what it was and discovered a pile of meat on the ground all cut up like stew meat, but I think it was pork with a lot of fat. It was a little tainted and didn't smell real good and flies had laid some eggs on it which would have turned into maggots later, but they hadn't reached that stage yet.

To us it was like Christmas, as everyone jumped into the act, washing and rinsing the meat several times and chopping the fat into even smaller pieces to render it and make cracklings and to have some lard to cook with later. The meat we turned into a delicious stew and it was a feast such as we hadn't had in a long time, all because Papa was tired of being hungry all the time. We went back a few other times, but we never got that lucky again. The Americans must have found a different dumping ground for their waste.

Another time we did get lucky in a different way and at a different place when we found a pile of folding Army cots the Americans had left behind on the golf course near Bad Kissingen where they had a camp for a while. We picked out six of the best ones and hauled them back to Euerdorf on a borrowed cart and they became the start of our new household and we actually ended up sleeping on them for several years, first on sacks filled with straw and later on used mattresses also discarded by the Americans.

Mama was desperate to move back to Wurzburg, and Papa had to get back because that was where his job was. The railroad had been at a complete standstill and nothing was moving at all in those waning days of World War II. A lot of the railroad system had been destroyed, but once the Americans had rolled through and the war was coming to an end, Papa needed to get back to work one way or the other.

Wurzburg was at least thirty miles away and there was no transportation and the only way to get there was on foot. So, early one morning Papa, Mama and Tante Marie headed out for Wurzburg. They walked all day long and by evening they had reached their destination. Papa stayed behind, moving in with our grandma and grandpa who were occupying one of Hanni's rooms.

Mama and Tante came walking back to Euerdorf, not too happy at all. There was no place for us to live in Wurzburg. Two different families had moved into four of Tante's rooms, moving all her left-behind things into the two remaining rooms, which were now wall-to-wall furniture, a totally unexpected development.

The cleanup of Wurzburg was already well on its way, a massive undertaking that would take many people and yet the infrastructure and supply system simply wasn't in place to accommodate so many people. So, the city was very selective about who was allowed to come back. Only able-bodied people who could wield a shovel were welcome. Anyone not willing to work on cleaning up the city didn't get a ration card and this meant almost certain death of starvation.

Our Karola and cousin Betty walked to Wurzburg and immediately were put to work clearing rubble from the streets. Papa was helping to clear tons of rubble at the railroad so it could begin functioning again. In the summer, our grandma and grandpa decided to move to Tuckelhausen, where our great grandma was still living, letting us have Hanni's room so we could move back to Wurzburg and be together again.

Mama walked back and forth another time or maybe even twice more before all the paperwork was completed and we could become legal citizens of Wurzburg again (Germans are a tightly controlled and structured people and are big on paperwork.). I have no recollection of how we got our cots and other belongings and ourselves to Wurzburg and apparently it wasn't as traumatic as when we left.

Hanni's room became our living room, bedroom, kitchen, washroom and everything else. More than four months had gone by since that awful night in March that changed everything. But we were glad to know that all of our extended family had also survived, most of them actually had less damage than our grandparents and us, who had lost everything. In December, the family who had shared the second floor of the "kirschbaum" with Hanni moved away, so we got their three rooms and things were looking up for us.

Papa had been collecting old boards and even straightened old, burned nails so he could nail together some furniture for us. Everyone was always out "scrounging" for anything usable, even sifting through the ashes, but because of the intense heat the bombing and firestorms had generated, very little was found. We were lucky that we had saved our good china and silverware, which now became our everyday china. Mama just wished she had put some pots and pans in the basement too. And we missed our feather beds desperately in that cold, drafty house we were living in up on the hill.

One of the families in the little house moved away as well, so Tante Marie was able to come back with Rudi, Gertie, and Peterle as well as Karola and Marita who had been living with the family Karola knew in Euerdorf. Betty had come back earlier, and by year's end everyone was back in Wurzburg and we celebrated a very quiet, subdued Christmas Eve together. We even had a small tree decorated with Mama and Papa's very first homemade ornaments that had been to Russia and back in 1943 before the war got really bad.

Karl had asked for some ornaments to decorate his little tree while stationed in Russia. He had sent them back but Tante had forgotten to give them back to Mama at the time. They seemed like old friends now, and really came in handy when we got them back, since all the carefully polished and preserved ornaments and icicles along with Papa's beautiful manger and the record player with all the records he had collected one by one were all gone now. But we tried not to dwell on that.

It was snowing softly as we all walked to midnight Mass at the church an hour's walk away (and the Mass really was at midnight back then). We knew there wouldn't be any presents under the tree so we hadn't even bothered to look and yet we felt peace and joy in our hearts—it was Christmas. Jesus was born! When we got back, lo and behold, there were two tiny little packages under the tree for Karin and me. They contained little silver charm bracelets, the prettiest things we had ever seen! Santa, or in our case, the Christkind, hadn't forgotten us after all.

Strangely enough, even though this whole ordeal we had experienced together had brought everyone closer to each other, it had also put a little crack into the wonderful, close relationship Mama had had with her sister, Tante Marie. Each one had their own private heartaches and thought the other one didn't show enough compassion and understanding for them. Mama would lament about all the things she had lost and Tante would point out that at least she still had all of us.

Tante had all her things, but her family was torn apart and she had lost all contact with her loved ones in Russia. In the end, only Uncle Willi came back, after seven or eight years in a Russian war prison. We never learned what happened to Max and Karl at all. We only learned of Arthur's fate because he died in a hospital in Breslau.

Thousands of men were "missing" in Russia and some of their wives had to have them declared legally dead after seven years to be able to get some assistance from the government for their children and to go on with their lives. It was not unusual for some men to come back after so many years of no contact only to find their wives had declared them dead and had remarried. There were messages scrawled on the ruins of Wurzburg informing those who were lucky enough to return from the war where they could find their loved ones. Those who were captured by the Americans and the British were the lucky ones, among them Hanni's husband Helm, as they were released and allowed to go home soon after the war ended.

Germany was carved up into four zones, controlled separately by the French, British, Russians and Americans. Once again, we were incredibly lucky that the Americans controlled our zone; their generosity and wealth were evident right from the beginning. It still took years because the devastation was so widespread, but of the four zones, the American zone recovered the quickest and surpassed all the others by far.

We would always be grateful for President Truman and his Marshall Plan and for not abandoning us when we needed help so desperately. Times would still be tough for several more years and hunger was still a big factor in our lives. Tragically, a mistake in translation was part of the cause of it.

When the German powers were asked what food they needed most to feed the people, they said "korn," a generic term for all grain, such as wheat, rye, oats, barley and those sorts of grains. The Americans took it literally and sent us tons of cornmeal that no one knew how to use, but it was part of our meager rations. Someone had figured out how many calories it took to keep us from starving to death and that is all we got.

In spite of everything Karin and I kept right on growing and soon we had outgrown everything in Karin's backpack that we had been sharing since I lost mine. Mama's sewing machine was gone, but she sewed what she could by hand out of the rags that had survived in the potato bin. I still remember the beautiful velvet skirt and bolero jacket with scalloped edges she made for me.

After two complete years of no formal schooling whatsoever, Schillerschule had rebuilt a few rooms for the children of Wurzburg, so we had to go. We were really nervous about it. I had only done part of fifth grade, but now I was in seventh grade—the second part of seventh grade actually, as the school year was half over already. But I soon discovered that we were all in the same boat as everyone else had forgotten everything they had ever learned as well.

For Mama it presented a whole new set of challenges too, as she had to come up with some kind of halfway decent clothing for us to wear and we had outgrown our shoes. We had to walk that same long, lonely road that Rudi had to walk when he went to Schillerschule, in all kinds of weather. Mama had somehow come by some really stiff, ugly brown army blankets that she had a seamstress turn into coats and pants for us, as they were too stiff for her to sew by hand. They turned out extremely ugly but we had to wear them to keep us warm so we had no choice. Papa had found a discarded, worn out pair of army boots in the ditch, which he turned into a pair of shoes for Karin, and I was able to wear Papa's leather tennis shoes he had kept in his backpack.

We were budding teenagers by then and sometimes we despaired at how ugly we felt. Money was pretty much useless. For once we had enough, but we couldn't buy anything with it. Black marketeering was rampant for American cigarettes or items of great value such as Persian rugs. One could "buy" just about anything on the black market, but we had nothing worthwhile to trade.

We were still using the money from Nazi times with swastikas printed on it, but no one wanted that. Sometime in 1948 or 1949, new bills had finally been printed but no one could get more than forty Marks and they had to give up four hundred of the old Nazi marks to get them. The money had been devalued ten to one. It took all of Papa's lifesavings for each of us to get 40 marks. Suddenly the stores were full of merchandise, but now we had no money again to buy anything.

Karin had half a year of eighth grade after the two-year lapse and then she was finished. The "Hauptschule" concept (free higher education for gifted children) was a Hitler program that wasn't available anymore. Karin tried everywhere to get an apprenticeship for any kind of job, but none were available. Most everyone we knew, including Mama, was working for the Americans, who paid better than the Germans and had jobs galore, but one had to be eighteen to work for them, and those who spoke English got even better jobs.

Then we learned that some Catholic nuns, "the Ursulines," were opening a finishing school for girls. Anyone who had finished seventh grade was welcome to apply. This of course included both Karin and me and we both passed the entrance exam in spite of our minimal school background (it was a pretty easy exam). The response was a lot greater than they had expected, but they tried to accommodate as many girls as possible.

Karin and I actually became classmates along with 50 or 60 other girls, some quite a bit older than I. It worked out very well for us. I became Karin's walking "memory" when she forgot things like boring dates we had to memorize and she became my tutor for things I didn't quite get the first time. We had no books, so the nuns would cover the blackboards at night with tiny writing for all our lessons, and they would mimeograph sheets from some master copy of typewritten materials.

They were strict and they had rules about a lot of things such as "no pants," but since no one could buy stockings anywhere, we were allowed to wear our ugly pants. But, we had to wear a dress or skirt over them, making us feel even uglier.

The school charged tuition of course, but it was reasonable and because there were two of us, we even got a reduction. This is where we learned English and French along with math, bookkeeping, stenography and a host of other subjects, religion being one of them of course, along with proper manners. It was a finishing school that was supposed to prepare us to make a better life for ourselves—or maybe snatch a richer husband.

The building was still largely in ruins, so every so often, classes would be interrupted when a load of bricks arrived or a bunch of roof tiles was delivered and we would form a human chain to help unload it. The sisters were always so happy when these deliveries were made, and for us kids it was a welcome diversion.

Something very new to us and also very welcome was the school lunch program, a gift from the American people that would be delivered everyday in large kettles, steaming hot. It was usually some kind of stew or macaroni and cheese we were not familiar with, but it smelled and tasted wonderful and definitely helped our mental state and capacity for learning.

People who lived through those crazy, awful years know that Germany owes a very large debt of gratitude to America and its people. This became even clearer after we had gone to see a movie that was advertised as "a movie every German should see." It was the scariest, most disturbing movie any of us had ever seen and it would haunt us for a very long time. It was a documentary about what the British and the Americans found when they entered the concentration camps of Belsen-Bergen, Buchenwald, and Dachau.

Some people might think that the German people had to know about this, but they really didn't. It was one of the best-kept secrets ever. We were totally shocked and dismayed and felt outrage, fear and shame and a whole range of other emotions about the terrible cruelty and brutality of our fellow countrymen. The sight of all those dead bodies that Mama was afraid of was impossible to erase from our minds, and it still is. We thought we had suffered, until we saw that. Our suffering was nothing compared to what happened in those camps.

It left a stain on the German people that can never be erased and yet people were willing to forgive and willing to give us a helping hand to get back on our feet again, especially the Americans. It took years and years of hard work and sacrifice to rebuild Wurzburg and restore it to its former charm and beauty, street by street and building by building.

It has been restored and it is once again a beautiful, charming city. Lest anyone forget, every March 16th at 7:20PM, the church bells in Wurzburg start ringing and they ring for twenty minutes, the exact time of the bombing of Wurzburg, one of the great tragedies of World War II.

Karin and I eventually did end up working for the Americans and that made a better life for us in so many ways. Through our workplace and different circumstances, we met our future husbands who were American servicemen and we came to live in America, where Karola, our big sister, a "war bride," had been living for many years already. We were so grateful for the opportunity to come here and build our lives and our families. We love America, the greatest country in the world and wouldn't want to live anywhere else. God bless America!

About The Author

Rosemarie Scheller was born March 23, 1934 in Wurzburg, Germany where she grew up during World War II. She was the youngest of three daughters born to Christian and Elizabeth Scheller, whose families had lived in that region of Germany for many generations. She, along with the rest of her extended family endured the struggles and deprivations of war and its aftermath on a country and its citizens who lost everything. After the war, Rosemarie married Wallace Rowan, an American service-man. They moved to the United States in 1956 and together they had four children. After raising her children and achieving the goal of seeing them all through college, Rosemarie worked for a number of years. Since her husband had been in the Air Force, they moved frequently and Rosemarie endured long periods of being away from her family and her dear sister Karin. Rosemarie's constant companion throughout her life was her sister Karin and for many years they had dreamed of sitting down together and writing their memoirs of those terrible times and how they made the best of them. She had never written anything other than letters before and her sister loathed writing. Sadly, her sister passed away before they could get started. Rosemarie decided to forge ahead on her own and wrote this in her sister's memory. For her, it was therapy to help with the grieving, and it was to give her children an appreciation of what life was like during the war. Rosemarie is now retired with Wallace, her husband of 50 years in Melbourne, Florida where she felt at peace enough with the loss of her sister to begin this project.